Character: The Heartbeat of the Novel

Third Edition

James R. Callan

Character: The Heartbeat of the Novel by James R. Callan

For information, contact the author through his website, www.jamesrcallan.com.
Character: The Heartbeat of the Novel
Third Edition, September 2021

What an Acquisition Editor Said about *Character: The Heartbeat of the Novel.*

"I am impressed, because this is absolutely the best book I've read so far on character development."

Ginnie Sienna Bivona, former Acquisition Editor, and Publisher.

What an Author Said about Character: The Heartbeat of the Novel.

"... an easy, enjoyable read with examples and suggested practice exercises. Assembled between the covers of this book are proven ways of bringing the protagonist and antagonist to life as real people the reader will love or despise and remember long after the novel has been returned to the shelf.

"This book is a gem that will fit in every author's reference library to be read and reread helping each of us to write that memorable novel we all dream and work toward creating."

Galand Nuchols, author of YA and middle grade reader books, including ***Lovely Lies, The Depth of Snow, Play the Cards You Are Dealt,*** **Different and Dangerous**, ***The Noose, Leroy's Chance, Second Chance***

Table of Contents

Introduction

Novels stand on three great pillars: Character, Plot and Dialog. All are essential to a good novel. Everyone agrees that without a good plot the novel is not going anywhere. And stilted dialog will discourage a reader from continuing. But often, the important work of developing memorable characters is overlooked or slighted.

Why is this?

The writer knows the characters, perhaps quite well, after spending months working with them. The reader, on the other hand, has just come on the scene. She doesn't know the characters and may not care about them. That's where the real work of the writer comes to the front. It is up to the writer to create memorable characters, characters the reader will care about, come to know and have feelings, good or bad, for the characters.

Consider a series. What ties a series together? What causes the readers to demand another book with – the same characters. They do not ask for the same plot. The readers have become friends (or enemies) with those characters and want to spend more time with them.

It is the character that will remain in the readers' memory long after the last page is finished.

Create a character that your reader loves and you'll have that reader hooked for every book in the series.

If you're not writing a series, memorable characters will encourage the reader to look for other books you have written, or will write.

So, the goal of this book is to help you create memorable characters that will attract a large and loyal fan base. Do the exercises. Follow the suggestions. You'll be on your way to *creating memorable characters.*

Chapter 1

We're # 1

Quite often, when a book title is mentioned, a person will say, "What was it about?" I know, not a good question, but they're really asking about the plot. So, Plot sticks up its finger and says, "We're number 1."

But when someone says, "I loved that book," and you ask why, or what did they like best about it, they will invariably say, "It had this great character." At that point, Character will claim, "We're number 1."

So, who's right?

Both Plot and Character are key components to determining whether a book is great, good, or terrible. Books exist that have no plot and yet are compelling. They are the exceptions, and they take an exceptional author. Then there are books whose plot is so engrossing that the fact the characters are not well drawn can be overlooked.

A good book needs both. Leave out the plot and the book goes nowhere. Like *Waiting for Godot*, you have only characters talking. They may bicker, but nothing happens. If you are Samuel Beckett, you can pull that off. But that leaves the rest of us looking for a plot.

Leave out a good character and the reader is likely to say, "Who cares?" You want your reader to identify with your protagonist, root for him or her, suffer along with the character when things aren't going well, and cheer when the protagonist triumphs.

People remember great characters. People tell other readers about a well-crafted character. It's like finding a new best friend. Well developed characters are the heart and soul of the book. When I took a poll some time ago, a riveting character was most often mentioned as the key to a good book.

Jack Bickham, creative writing professor at Oklahoma University for many years, in one of his books on writing has a chapter titled "Characters Make the Difference."

Aside from all that, the subject of this book is how to develop memorable characters. So, at least for now, I'm promoting Character to the number one spot, the top dog, that part of the novel we *must* develop with great care, with imagination, and with patience.

Memorable characters don't spring from the keyboard onto the screen, hop to the printer, and slither through the ether to the editor's computer. They must be crafted, honed, reworked, and adjusted until you, your editor, and most important, your reading public, love them. When you achieve that, you have crossed the line from writer to memorable writer.

Note: to avoid using "him/her," and "his/hers" and certainly to avoid using "them" when I'm only talking about one person, I will use the masculine form part of the time and the feminine form part of the time. Those are *not* intended to be gender specific.

Chapter 2

Put on Your Thinking Hat

Now, down to business.

Some authors start with a character and build the novel around this person. In this case, the character is usually the protagonist. But, it could be the antagonist. Who came first in *Hannibal*? I am not privy to Thomas Harris's thoughts. But, as Hannibal Lecter was featured in two previous Harris novels, notably *Silence of the Lambs*, it seems likely that the antagonist character of Lecter might have been the first character envisioned by Harris for *Hannibal* and probably *Silence of the Lambs.*

Other authors start with an incident and add the necessary characters. And still others may take a particular locale as the starting block for the novel. I like to have the inciting incident (which of course includes a principal character), and develop from there.

Whatever is used to start the process, the story has to have characters to people it. So, the author—that's you—begins to picture these people. You need to let these people take shape in your mind. You need to get to know them. At first, this is on a general level. How will they fit into the book? What is their role? Is this one going to be the protagonist? Is that one going to be the sidekick? Are they going to get along? The beginning of a relationship might start to emerge. What about the antagonist? Is the antagonist a person? Or not. (I'll discuss the non-person antagonist in chapter 20.)

Sometimes, the character pops up in your mind, fully grown, sticking out his or her hand and saying "Glad to meet you," or maybe, "Get out of my way, sleaze bag." For me, at least, it is more likely that the pictures of these players emerge slowly, coming into focus gradually like the old Polaroid pictures. Many authors find it helpful to actually find pictures in magazines or old albums that look similar to those pictures materializing in the author's mind. The author will cut those out, or make a photocopy, and put them on a poster board where other information germane to the book will get posted.

Probably you don't really know the character yet. But now you have a picture, literally or at least in your mind, and other qualities will begin to materialize. Regardless of how you have gotten to this point, it is helpful to let the characters percolate in your mind. You mull over them; they tumble together, and you begin to see the relationships.

Like good wine, the more time you can let this happen, let them ferment, the better the end product. This is where patience comes in. There is a tendency (that means, I do it) to rush this process. I'm ready to get this show on the road. Let's get moving; the bus is about to leave. But time spent in this phase will pay dividends down the road. A character well defined in your mind and on paper will make the writing of the book much easier. More important, it will make it a better book.

The good, the bad and the ugly

What about modeling your characters after real people you know? Obviously you will have a character that is real. After all, he or she came from a real person.

The first word that comes to my mind is – dangerous. This is rarely a good idea. Can you use a real person to *help* mold your character? Yes. This guides you to include various aspects that you might otherwise overlook. You get a feeling of confidence that this character is "real." Why not? You modeled it after a real person. Who is "realer" that old John over there, or Mary Sue?

But your character must not be a carbon copy. Sure, the person is flattered you will model a character after him if you tell him. That lasts until the book appears. He or she (I'll use he to keep it simple) eagerly grabs a copy. Most likely he expects you to *give* him a copy. After all, he did supply you with a leading character. (He would never expect you to use him for a minor character.) As he races through your book, looking for himself and how he made everything work out just right, the character doesn't look as good as the person pictures himself. Keep in mind, that you may have given the character qualities just a little better than your friend has. It makes him look better and juices up the book a bit. But when your friend reads it, the character just isn't as good as ... well, as your friend sees himself.

Trouble.

Or maybe it is too revealing and causes him undying trouble when other people read it. This may lead to you losing a friend. It could even end up in a law suit. If you haven't told him in advance, the situation could be worse. Ian Fleming was sued by Erno Goldfinger when Ian named one of his villains Goldfinger. The matter was settled out of court. Other authors have lost lawsuits when a person in their books had too many characteristics that matched the real person.

You also need to decide if what you are writing is libelous. If it is, cut it out. Keep in mind, the author is most likely the one who is sued and will pay if she or he loses the case.

Dead or Alive?

Is the person in the public eye? If so, you have more leeway. In most states, you can't libel a dead person. That doesn't mean his family won't cause you a lot of trouble and you may spend time in court, even if you don't lose the case. But certainly for live people, you should ask if putting this item in the book will cause the person any problems, real or imagined. And, ask yourself if you want to do that.

The key thing to remember when using a real person as the template for one of your characters is to change enough characteristics that it will not be clear you actually used that particular person. You can substitute for certain characteristics which are not essential to what you are trying to achieve. For instance, if you want a talented athlete, and it makes no difference, switch to a different sport. If that makes a difference, change his hair and eye colors. Switch right-handed to left-handed. If that makes a difference, give him a set of parents very different from the parents of your model. You do not need for every characteristic to be the same. Pick significant ones and change those that won't affect your story. Changing hair and eye color probably won't help you if you are sued, but it might dissuade the person from suing, particularly if the minor characteristic is emphasized. For instance, if you give the character red hair, and everybody calls him "Red" or "Carrot Top," that highlights this difference from the real person, even if most other aspects match pretty closely.

Remember, the goal of this book is to help you make a memorable character. John Updike won *two* Pulitzer Prizes for his character Harry "Rabbit" Angstrom. Yes, Updike wrote full books that the prize committee read. But Rabbit won the races and took the prizes. Memorable. Your mission, if you choose to accept it, is to create your own "Rabbit."

Exercise

1. Think of a character. It could be from a WIP (work in progress), or a work contemplated. It can be the protagonist,

antagonist, or the sidekick for the protagonist. It could be a minor character. But since we will visit this character several times, you might want to spend your time on a major character.

It is probably best not to use a character from a book already in print.

Make a few notes on this character. Then as we go through the rest of this book, we'll use that character for various exercises. So, exercise 1: jot down a very brief note on this character. We'll fill in the blanks later. For now, just make a brief note to reserve his or her place.

2. Did you ever have a character just come to you fully developed? If so, did that character change during the writing of the novel? If so, how did the character change?

Chapter 3

Setting the Bar

The character is beginning to take shape in your mind. Ask yourself, what do you want the character to achieve in this book? Before we get to the nitty-gritty aspect of describing this guy, think about his mission in life (your book). His mission will require certain characteristics, or you will need to explain how he overcomes the lack of these.

By deciding this early on, you can avoid having to go back and change some aspect of his makeup. Certainly you can go back and make changes, but we're trying to avoid such. Each time you go back and adjust part of this character you risk causing other problems. And when you address those issues, you risk entering new obstacles. Some of these will surface at the end and can be corrected during rewrite. Others will come to light when readers tell you about the inconsistencies. Not a good time. You want your *characters* memorable, not your *mistakes*.

We've all heard about characters taking on a life of their own as the book progresses. This can happen. In fact, if you develop your characters well enough, this should happen. They will speak to you. So you also need to ask what goals might this character come up with on his own. Then, as you develop the character, allow for those goals.

Another option is to say, "I am the author and only I decide what happens in this book, not one of the characters." Of course, this later approach might cause the character to be less interesting than if you give the character his head and let him decide some of the issues. It's your choice.

My opinion is this. You will be working on this novel for months. You will know the characters. But the characters are *living* in this story. If they have a suggestion on how things should go, it makes sense to listen to them. You do not have to agree, or follow their suggestions. But you should pay attention to them, consider what they have to say, and then decide whether to accept their idea, or not.

Example: Linda Apple, a well-published Oklahoma author, once wrote that she was finished with a book when one of the characters said, "One of my characters tapped my creative shoulder and said 'You are not finished yet. My story has to be fleshed out. You just skimmed by me and that doesn't fly with me.'" Linda looked over the book and decided the character was right. She paid attention to what the character had to say. And, the author said the book got better by doing so.

Lions and tigers and bears! Oh my!

What does your character fear? Nothing? Even Superman feared Kryptonite. You character fears something. It might be his father, his mother, his older brother. It might be fear of failure, or fear of being afraid, fear of snakes. Find out what he fears. This will shape some of his decisions. This will color his view of others. This might help determine what *his* goal is.

Example: In the Hitchcock movie Vertigo, James Stewart, because of an accident in the line of duty, has acrophobia (an extreme fear of heights). It is a key element in the story. A character's fear can help the author.

I was very young, ...

Was there something in your character's early life that helps shape her life today? This does not have to be something bad, although it often is. Perhaps she was abused. This could be physical or emotional. In grade school she might have been labeled as very nice but a bit dull. She might, in fact be exceptionally smart, but this label has led her to set very low goals for herself, to have a low self-esteem, to avoid conversations with people she deemed to be smart. Certainly there have been cases where a very smart child tries to look below average to "fit in," to avoid the label of "just a brain."

It can be as simple as being taller than everybody else. Others, particularly the boys who are ashamed that a girl is taller than they are, will make fun of her, play horrible jokes on her, put her down at every opportunity. Does this stay with her for the rest of her life? It can. Or she might overcome it. Or she thinks she has overcome it and then something happens to bring it all back. She may recognize it, or she may not. But her reaction to a person she meets might have been determined twenty years earlier.

Of course, this early shaping incident could be something very positive. Her elderly aunt took in an unkempt vagrant off the street, fed him, gave him some almost new clothes her late husband had bought just before his untimely death, and provided the vagrant with money for a bus ticket to some place he wanted to go. The aunt had never seen him before and never saw him again. Your character, an eleven year old girl at the time, was greatly affected by this show of generosity to a complete stranger. Now, your character has as her goal to be as kind and generous to others as possible. Occasionally she is taken advantage of, but that does not dissuade her.

You do not necessarily need to describe this early-life incident in detail, or at all. But it provides motivation for various acts of your character. If you know about the incident, you will understand your character better, realize why certain choices are made. In effect, you are able to create a "real" character, one worth remembering.

As I see it ...

How do others in your book view the character? Do they view her as she really is, or as the person she *thinks* she is, which might be very different? At times, jealousy can cause others to put down your character. If she has some self-doubt, this will be reinforced.

It can also work the other way. In *Being There*, a satirical novel by Jerzy Kosinski, circumstances put a simple minded gardener in with an adviser to the President of the United States. The advisor does not know Chance is a gardener, and believes him to be a highly educated business man. When Chance has no idea what he has been asked, he resorts to the only thing he knows, gardening. The President and his advisors believe Chance is speaking allegorically, and decide he has the best political mind around. Those around Chance have given him much better qualities than he has in reality. In his simple mind, these roll off him with no effect. But in a different situation (your book, maybe), the character could believe these false, enhancing qualities and either live up to them or become disillusioned when he can't.

This brings us to a very important point. You must know how the character views herself. Does she see herself as others see her? Does she have trouble when people treat her or describe her in a way that differs from her own self image? Remember the girl a few paragraphs back who was told she was dull. Does she still see herself that way? What happens when others see her differently? How will she react when her boss wants to give her more important assignments? Does she see them as a challenge, or does it cause her to shrink, refuse to take them, or experience emotional stress? Perhaps she will not even try to do the job she is capable of, because she doesn't see herself as being that capable. There is always the possibility that she will work twice as hard, knowing she isn't capable, but wanting to please the boss. She does a fantastic job and finally, at last, she realizes she is capable of good work; she can finally see for herself that she is not dull.

Exercises

1. Take the character you noted in the exercise from chapter 2 and give him or her a goal to achieve in the book. Then, take a moment to decide what it is the character fears.

2. Was there anything in the character's youth that will come back to play a part in the book? This may be the root of the character's fear. Was it real or imagined?

3. Could this fear, and how he deals with it in the current circumstances, actually lead to his achieving his goal in the book? And could this incident banish his fear for all time?

Chapter 4

A Rose by Any Other Name Would Still Have Thorns

Picking names for your characters is important. Please don't pick up the telephone directory (if they still have those where you live) and select names at random. The right name can shape your character. The right name can set the reader on the right path. The reader immediately has an impression of who this character is, what this character is about.

Consider the characters in the Harry Potter books by J. K. Rowling. Sirius Black, Ron Weasley, Griiphook, Nymphadora Tonks, Severus Snape, Albus Dumbledore, Draco Malfoy, Luna Lovegood, Dobby, Argus Filch, Gregory Goyle, Cornelius Fudge. Clearly, she didn't use my phone book. Those names didn't just pop off her tongue. Considerable thought went into them. Even the figures in the paintings had names.

It paid off. The names in the Harry Potter books have in themselves sparked great interest and prompted a number of books. When the publisher asked people which was their favorite name in the Potter books, 70,000 people voted. (Severus Snape won.) Do 7,000 people care about the names in your books? Do 700 make a comment on any of your names?

You can select a name that compliments some characteristic of the character. Auric Goldfinger, courtesy of Ian Fleming, certainly gave us some insight into the antagonist of a book originally titled *The Richest Man in the World*. Matt Baron, principal character in Jory Sherman's *Grass Kingdom* has many of the qualities we might associate with a baron. Donn Taylor's book *Deadly Additive* has a character named Brinkman, who operates on the brink. Was that name an accident? I think not.

Margaret Mitchell originally called her protagonist in *Gone with the Wind* Pansy. Would we have found her as memorable as Scarlett O'Hara? Do we start with a different picture or impression of the character named Pansy than we do with one named Scarlett?

When we read about Sam Spade, we immediately have a predisposition on his character. A Spade is a no-nonsense piece of hardware made for hard work.

We don't expect Holly Golightly to be a research historian spending her time in a dusty library back room.

We don't expect Darth Vador to be a standup comic.

Would you have a different feeling about a character named Catherine if she calls herself Cat? And what would that say about her own feeling about herself, her self image?

Names count.

The name can also be a contrast to the character. By the way, this attention to names can, and should, include the names of fictitious places. David Baldacci in his book *Divine Justice* names a town "Divine" to contrast the true nature of the place.

Some names tell us about the ethnic background of a person. Kelly O'Rourke is probably not an Israeli. A nick name is usually very telling. Of course, the nick name may have been a very apt description of the person when a teenager and may not apply now. Still, it gives the reader some background.

Times change ... and so do names ...

I had a complaint once about the name of one of my characters. The complaint was that at the time the character was born, the name I'd given him was not at all popular, rarely if ever used. How was I to know? The answer was simple. There is a website where you can look back at any year after 1879 and find the most popular names for boys and for girls. So, you might want to check and see if that name was used at the time your character would have been born.

If I've outlawed the phone book as a name bank, where *is* a good source of names? One place that will give you the popular names by decade or year all the way back to 1879 is the Social Security Administration. At www.ssa.gov/oact/babynames you can select a year and get a list of the most popular names for babies born in that year. So, if your character was born in 1952, she had a good chance of being named Linda. Ashley, on the other hand, didn't make the top 500 most popular names. The most popular girl's name last year was Olivia. (When the first edition of *Character: The Heartbeat of the Novel* was published, the most popular girl's name for babies was Sophia. Last year, Sophia was ranked 5th.) But if your character was born in 1960, Sophia might not be a good choice. It didn't make the top 500. Unless, of course, you wanted to make the point that her parents chose to be different, and perhaps raised their daughter to be different.

You can also get the most popular names by state, and this does vary widely from one state to another.

Another site, www.babynames.com , will give you the meanings and origins of names. Soome sites also provide names by categories, such as "old lady names," or "billionaire names," (Cash might be a good name for a male billionaire) or names by a theme, such as exotic names or biblical names or bird or flower names. You might use the meaning of the name to give a clue to your character's nature. www.babynameworld.com also gives the meanings of names. For instance, Sophia means wisdom.

The site http://www.kabalarians.com/index.cfm is a website that gives lists of names and the character traits that often go with a person with that name.

And there is www.babynames.co.uk if you want a more British name.

Of course, you can make up a name. It is permissible to name your child whatever you wish. Consider Frank Zappa's children, Moon Unit and Dweezil, or Actress Shannyn Sossamon's son Audio Science. So you can most certainly name your characters anything you like. However strange the name you come up with seems, probably somebody has already named a child that very name.

Variety is the Spice of Life.

I try to avoid having any two names close together in sound or spelling. I don't want Joe and Joey confused, or Mary and Marty confused, or Missy and Misty, or Sam and Cam. I hate it when a novel has three main female characters and their names are Jane, Joan and Jean. I almost have to get a piece of paper and write down, "Jane is the neighbor to the left – oh, that's left if you stand in the street and look at the houses."

Some of you will think I am being anal, which may just mean you know me better than others. But I try not to have names of any main male characters start with the same letter. The same is true for the major female characters. For instance, in my novel *Cleansed by Fire*, I have eight main male characters. Their names started with the letters B, E, F, H, M, S, T and W. And none of the names are close together in sound. You're right—anal. But I want to make it easy for my readers to keep the characters straight. I hate for a reader ever to have to go back and try to figure out who's who. Was it Tim or Jim who picked up that package? Did Cecelia or Celestia own a gun?

So, what's in a name? It's up to you. You can make it be just a place-holder, a way to distinguish one character from another. If this is your bent, you can save yourself a lot of trouble and just name them A, B, C, D, and so on. But, if you want to write a good novel with interesting, *memorable* characters, take the time to find a significant name for your characters—at least your major characters. It's just another piece of the puzzle to make your characters memorable. And that is our goal.

Exercises

1. Pick a name for your protagonist. Spend a few minutes to come up with a "good" name. If you're not sure what I mean by a "good" name, go back and read the chapter again. Note, I said a few minutes. This is not a ten second exercise – unless you've already been thinking about it. Explain why you have chosen this name

2. Now pick a name for your antagonist. Does his name suggest he is a bad guy? Or maybe he has a name that makes him sound like an angel. Are you trying to misdirect the reader, making it not obvious this is the bad guy? Explain why you have chosen this name.

3. Since I think the sidekick character can be a great help to the author, devote a few minutes to selecting a good name for the sidekick. It can be a nick-name, a formal name, or a more friendly name. But, think about how you picture the sidekick and select the name carefully. And remember, you can change the name midway through writing. Just be careful to make certain it is changed everywhere. It is very confusing to the reader if a character's name gets changed but some instances of the former name get left in the book.

Chapter 5

It's Your Galatea–Time to Sculpt Your Protagonist

Back in 1884, Edwin Abbott Abbott wrote a novel entitled *Flatland: A Romance of Many Dimensions*. When I was in graduate school, studying mathematics, it was popular. (No, that was not in 1884.) The story is about the two-dimensional world of Flatland. The women are simple line-segments while the men are polygons, and the narrator is a humble square. It is an interesting story but I won't go into the plot. Write if you want more details on *Flatland*, it's on Amazon in paper and Kindle editions. Written in 1884 and on Kindle. Amazing, isn't it?

If you are going to write a sequel to *Flatland*, then you can get away with one and two dimensional characters. Good luck on finding a publisher. But for the rest of us, we're not writing *Flatland* and we cannot get away with two dimensional characters.

According to Greek mythology, Galatea was a statue carved by Pygmalion that came to life. Now, it's time for you to begin to sculpt your Galatea. It's time for you to create a character so well, so complete, so believable that the character will come to life.

The word for the day is "**Eccentric**."

The primary definition of eccentric is "not having the same center." This is followed by "deviating from the norm." It helps to have an eccentric character, one who deviates from the norm. You can write about a person who is perfectly normal in every respect, but who will remember him? He's like everybody else. If he looks and acts like the rest of the people around him, how can you pick him out?

Think of the Irish story about the leprechaun who is captured. To obtain his release, he has to tell his captor where the leprechaun's pot of gold is hidden. He tells the man that it is buried at the base of a tree and promises to tie a yellow ribbon around the tree if the man will free him. The man releases the leprechaun and the next morning goes to the forest. To his dismay, every tree has a yellow ribbon tied around it. The leprechaun has kept his promise. But the man has no idea which tree is the right one.

If your character looks like every other character, how can we remember your character? Remember our goal: *create memorable characters.*

So, write "eccentric" on a card and post that on your board. William Doonan's *Grave Passage* has an octogenarian detective who falls asleep. He forgets things. But *you* remember him. Dan Brown's *Da Vinci Code* features Robert Langdon, a famous symbologist (one who studies symbols). That's different. Sandra Brown develops an antagonist who likes to reenact movie murder scenes. Eccentric. Lisa Brackman, in *Rock, Paper, Tiger*, has a Viet Nam veteran with PTSD. But her character is a female. That's different. Back when she published the book, most of the stories dealing with PTSD center on male vets.

Bill Fitzhugh, in *Pest Control*, has Protagonist Bob, a household pest exterminator. A man from Paris hires Bob the exterminator, thinking he's an assassin. Now, international assassins decide Bob is jumping their claim and come after Bob. That's a bit different.

Another word to post on your board today is "**exaggerate**."

Take a lesson from the leprechaun. If your character looks, sounds, acts like everyone else, not only will she not stand out, she'll be lost in the woods. This is your Galatea; sculpt her any way you want, but make her exceptional—one way or another. Exaggerate.

Author and creative writing instructor Jack Bickham says, "**Exaggeration is the first step toward creating vivid fictional characters.**"

One of my all-time favorite characters is Cyrano de Bergerac, the protagonist in the Edmond Rostand play of the same name. Everything about him is larger than life. He is a remarkable swordsman who composes a ballade while dueling with a nobleman. Later, Cyrano's friend tells him a hundred men are waiting to kill him. Cyrano takes them on and complains that there are not a hundred. Cyrano has a very large nose, one he says "marches on before me by a quarter of an hour."

He is larger than life. Is he exaggerated? Certainly. Is he memorable? Most definitely.

Metaphor? Simile?

What are those two doing in my discussion of character development? They're tools to help you make your character stand out. Suppose I say, "John had big ears." (Yeah, I know. Poor choice for a name.) I can do better. "John had large ears." Nope. No better. "John had huge ears." A tiny bit better. "John's ears looked like weather balloons attached to his head." That's a **simile** - comparing two things which are dissimilar items, such as comparing ears to weather balloons, and using the word "like" or "as." Which description are you going to remember?

"Mano's hand was a catcher's mitt." **Metaphor** is the comparison of two things that are in general not alike, without using "like" or "as." The reader knows this guy didn't really have a catcher's mitt for a hand. But the reader knows very clearly, this guy had big hands, exceptionally big hands. Your reader will remember that feature about him. You, the author, can use that fact later in the book to good advantage. And guess what? The reader will remember.

Examples:

"Her eyes were like sapphires cut to catch the light and sparkle." Simile.

"His eyes were lasers, the kind that cut through steel." Metaphor.

"He was only five feet tall, but his feet were as big as a seven foot giant's." Simile.

His two feet were a yard. Metaphor

Can you overdo the use of metaphor and simile? You most certainly can. They should be used like the habañero: not on everything, and not too much. (Simile.)

Pay attention ...

I hear someone saying, "I only know boring people. Nobody in my circle of acquaintances has such startling eyes. Or ears or hands or feet, for that matter."

First, I seriously doubt that. Take a closer look. I used to think that. But I found I wasn't really seeing the people, wasn't really listening to them, wasn't paying attention. It is impossible to be a writer if you do not observe life around you. These people have been around you long enough that you don't even see the exceptional features.

Second, spend your time in the airport, restaurant, shopping mall, or political rally looking at all the people who are passing by. Keep a pad of paper and a pencil handy. Jot down a few words of description about interesting people you see. And hear. Listen to how they interact with those around them, their traveling companions, eating partner, store clerk, or precinct head. You will be amazed at how many interesting, eccentric, and exaggerated characteristics people have.

I was sitting in the airport waiting for my flight to board. A short Mexican with a grey beard that reached below his waist walked by. He had mean eyes. And he held one of his hands hidden behind the beard. I made a note and sure enough, he appeared in my book *A Ton of Gold.* By the way, I am not putting down Mexicans. I find them to be happy, energetic people. We have a home in Mexico. But, this man had eyes like a junk-yard dog—mean.

And third, your characters are not real people. Not yet, anyway. I hope, after you finish this book, you will make your characters "real." Real, but eccentric. Exaggerated. Take a skeleton character, based on some actual person you see or know, and then sculpt a memorable character by adding, subtracting, adjusting. Apply a little metaphor here, a little simile there. Exaggerate a bit here, make her a little—or a lot—eccentric there.

What can you exaggerate? Everything. Her smile can be brighter, sassier, more infectious, or more sinister than anybody else's. His anger can be worse than the Hulk's. His physical attributes can top even Sly Stallone's. Her dress can put cover girls to shame. Physical, mental, emotional, whatever you can say about a character, you can exaggerate. Think Cyrano. My nose "marches on before me by a quarter of an hour." I rather doubt that. But here I am, forty years later, remembering the exact line that exaggerated a feature of a character.

When I attempted to paint, I tried to make it look like a photo, exactly like the real thing. I failed at that. But even if I had succeeded, I would not have been an artist. I had set the wrong goal. A good painter tries to capture more than is visible to the camera's eye. He tries to bring out what is hidden: perhaps character, personality, intellect, feeling, something a camera won't pick up. Your characters are your painting, your statue. You don't want a photograph, an exact replica. You want something better—more memorable.

Do not fear overdoing it. In fact, strive to overdo it. You can tone it down during the rewrite. Most of the time, you won't want to, won't need to. You will come to love the character as is. No change necessary. Often, it is the very characteristic that you thought was over the top when you first wrote it that now causes you to smile every time that character strides onto the page. It's like (simile) when I bake. I try to overdo the pecans. I decide what is enough, and then I double the amount. And sometimes I say, "I've done it this time. I've finally put in too many pecans." But guess what? When the item comes out of the oven, it never has too many pecans.

Personification. This is more difficult but can be very effective when used carefully. In personification, you give human qualities to an action, a feeling, or a non-human thing.

Example: Jim could hear the peach cobbler calling him.

Exercises

1. This may take more than a few minutes. Give your character something that you can exaggerate. Use a metaphor to describe this.

2. Again, give one of your characters some facet you can exaggerate. Use a simile to describe this aspect of the character.

3. Again, plan on spending a little time on this. Take a major character — protagonist, antagonist, or sidekick — and give him

or her an eccentric characteristic. Make it something that fits the character, works in smoothly, but will make the character memorable.

4. This time, take a minor character and give that character something eccentric associated with him or her. It could be some part of his personality, or something he has experienced or done in his life, or perhaps some unusual phrase he often uses.

5. Try to use personification in some situation with your sidekick.

Chapter 6

Even the CIA Doesn't Know This Much About Her.

One way or another, you must have bios. When a writer tells me he does not make bios, I know he means he does not write out a long file on the computer. But he has a bio. It may be in his head. Most likely some of that is on paper, or in a file. Maybe it's only a scrap of paper. Maybe it's the result of hours of thinking about this character.

I guess it sometimes happens that a character pops into your head fully formed and ready for prime time.

Don't wait for that to happen.

There are pantsers, those who write by the seat of their pants. That is, they get an idea and plunge right in and let the story go where the characters lead them. They probably do not do bios, at least not on paper or in the computer. But it is likely that even pantsers have a mental bio for the protagonist and antagonist.

The reality is, if you are writing long books, you need a written bio you can refer to from time to time. Did I say her eyes reminded one of aged bronze? (Stolen from my book *A Ton of Gold.*) Will I remember that months from now when I write the final scene of the sequel and want to refer to her eyes? Probably not. If next year, I write the third in the series, am I going to remember? Do I have to go back and read four chapters to find out how I described her eye color?

Not me. I'm going to pull up the bio on Crystal and in five seconds I've got it. Oh, and I forgot. She was five feet eight, not five feet nine. If I put in five feet nine, some reader will write to me and say, "Did she really grow an inch taller after she was thirty?" And then I have to answer, "Nice to hear from you and so happy you remembered how tall Crystal was." It's embarrassing when the reader knows more about the character than the author does.

Those of you with perfect recall, who never forget anything, can skip this. For the rest of us, let's proceed.

Let's get serious. Not all bios are created equal. Your bio for the protagonist, the sidekick, and the antagonist should be extensive, complete. They should contain more information that you will use. The bios for minor characters will contain much less information.

Lest we forget ...

Even for minor characters, I want something written down. How/why did they get into this novel? I even like to keep track of *where* they entered. If I have to go back and make any changes in or about this character, I want to know just how far back I need to go. If you write the book in three weeks, this may not be a problem. But if you take months to finish the book, and then months to polish it, such knowledge may get fuzzy. You can save yourself a lot of time with a simple file. Keep in mind, this is for you only. So it doesn't have to be well polished, just neat enough and complete enough so that you can do a quick search. *Ah ha, Jill entered to help Jack carry the water back in chapter 3*.

You might find it helpful if all the bios follow the same organization. The short bios will leave out many sections, but the general flow will be similar. That could be something like this, but feel free to organize it in a way it makes sense to you.:

Role in this book
Physical description
Tells (see chapter 15 for a description of a tell.)

Dress
Family
Friends
Current living place or arrangement
Transportation
How do others see this character
How does the character see herself
Locations
Education
Job path
Health
Likes
Dislikes
Strengths
Weaknesses
Goals
Hobbies
Fears
Psychological aspects
Early life episodes that influenced (this could include any back-story information)
Significant change during this book
Etc.

For the protagonist, antagonist, and the sidekick you may fill in most of those slots, with lots of details. Keep in mind, this will be a *dynamic* bio. You will add to it as the book progresses and you find that you need more information. Perhaps at the beginning, you haven't needed any childhood experiences. Later, you need something to provide the motivation for a particular act. *Ah ha, he had a sled when he was six, and he called it Rosebud.* Since this is a computer file, it's a snap to open the file and add that info in.

Hobbies can tell a lot about a character. Suppose your female protagonist keeps piranhas as a hobby? Does that say a lot about her? Or a young man reads the dictionary. What about a girl who enters every beauty contest, large or small, within her travel area, but never even places? Each of these shows the reader a lot about the character. And when did the person first begin this hobby? A life-long hobby? Did she start it after something changed in her life? Or maybe she took it up last week.

Naturally, these hobbies must fit in with the true nature of the character. Don't put in some outrageous hobby just to get noticed. If it doesn't work for the character, the reader will know you are not being true to that character. Of course, the point could be made in the book, perhaps by the sidekick, that this hobby does not fit this person. What's going on? Why did she take this up?

Family seems pretty fixed, but not always. As the book progresses you may need additional family members. Open the bio and put them in, and at the same time, you can make certain that this new family member fits in properly with the rest of the family and doesn't have the same name – unless that's an important fact.

For a minor character, you may include physical description, skip to health if it matters, and include what chapter this character first appeared. As with the major characters, you can add to this as the book progresses and as needed.

In the next chapters, we'll look closely on how to construct a long bio for a major character, and a shorter bio for a sidekick character. Following those chapters, you'll find blank copies of long and short bios that you can copy and use as a template for your characters.

Exercise

You get a break on this chapter: no exercise. We'll save it for after chapter 8.

Chapter 7

Once and Done, or Many Returns

One of the first things that would be nice to know (but not essential) is whether this character will be a series character, or a stand-alone character. What do I mean by that?

Do you envision this character as one who will appear in a number of your books? That could be a series of books which are connected by the same protagonist or by the same central theme. The same locale generally is not sufficient, in and of itself. It could also be that you will use this character in other books which do not form a series. He or she could be the protagonist in this book and possibly only a minor character in another book. The point is, you believe you will use this character again.

Or do you expect that this character will never show up in one of your books again? Naturally, you reserve the right to bring a character back. But what are your plans at present? Do you expect this to be a one night stand for this character? Or maybe the character dies in this book.

Why do you care?

If you plan to use this character in a series, you must give special attention to the various aspects of the character. You will be stuck with those for future books. By that I mean, your readers will remember (if you've made a memorable character – the goal of this book). So, you can't change many of those.

Example: If he is definitely anti-smoking in book one, the reader doesn't want to see him puffing away on a long cigar in book 2. Could he be a smoker in book one and very anti-smoking in book two? Absolutely. But you should explain that. He lost his best friend to lung cancer and now is on a mission to stamp out smoking. Or his doctor told him he will die within a year if he keeps up his three-pack-a-day habit.

Example: Suppose in book one, he has a bad limp because he was born with one leg shorter than the other. If you want to make him a sprinter trying out for the Olympics in book two, it just won't play. Don't make him a tournament tennis player in book one, and then in the next book want him to overcome a life-long medical problem that has kept him from any strenuous activity.

These are extreme and obvious cases. That's to make the point that there can be problems if you do not give careful thought to all of the qualities you give a character. Of course, you want to think things through clearly on any character, one time or multi-appearance. But, a characteristic that might be good for the once and done character, might not be the best idea for the repeat performer.

Exercise

1. Decide if you think this character you've chosen will be a one-book stand, or an on-going relationship.

2. Think of a character that you might well use in future books. List a few things that will need special attention to avoid problems in the next book in which the character appears.

Chapter 8

A Road Map

I've talked about bios and how important they are. I've suggested long bios for the major characters and short bios for minor characters. I've said that these bios are dynamic. By that I mean that you will update them as the book progresses. And I've said that you will/should refer to them frequently as you write the book.

Please note, these are not to restrict you, the writer. They are not to hamper your creative nature. They do not keep the character from growing. That's why they are dynamic—they allow the character to grow. But at the same time, they keep your character true. They prevent you from making mistakes or inconsistencies. They help you with the motivation of the character. They encourage you to create three dimensional characters. This is not *Flatland*.

- Bios are a help, not a hindrance.

- Time spent on bios is not a waste.

Do not feel like they are slowing you down. On the contrary, they allow you to write better, faster, because you know the character so well. You know how she will react to a particular situation, what she is likely to say, which path she will take. It makes you knowledgeable, better prepared to flow through this novel without looking over your shoulder, wondering, "Have I made a mistake on this character? Would she really react that way? Would she really say that?"

On the other hand, the bio does not keep the character from growing, changing, evolving as the book progresses. What the bio does do is keep the character true to herself. When a character takes on a life of its own, you don't want it to be phony. And if the character is so strong-willed that it must go in a different direction, then you just have to go back and adjust the bio to make certain your readers don't say, "Based on the first half of the book, this doesn't work. The author has suddenly given me a different character. He doesn't match up."

This could happen if that character has a split personality, has been exposed to an atomic radiation disaster, or if a piece of a mysterious asteroid landed in his backpack and he carried it around for days without noticing. If so, know what you're doing. And let the reader know. And your bio has a before and after section for this character.

If I've convinced you that bios are good, let's look at a long bio of a fictitious character in a novel that I am contemplating. I'm going to pull out all the stops here and this bio will probably be longer than you end up doing for your protagonist. Or maybe not. Here we go. (Note: When I do the bio, I am not going to worry about complete sentences, or even spelling for that matter. Just the facts, ma'am.)

Example:

Bio for Holly Highroad

Roll in this book

- What is the roll in this book for this character? Protagonist, antagonist, sidekick, other relationship to the book or other major character?

Physical:

- Female, five feet six inches tall 115 pounds
- Chestnut hair
- Eyes: brown with a yellow speck or two in each eye.
- She wears contacts much of the time, but when studying or grading papers she has a small pair of reading glasses.
- She does not like her nose, but she won't succumb to cosmetic surgery. She just endures it. Actually, it's not bad at all, but still shows the slight effects of being broken when she was ten.
- She has a slender build, Reasonable figure. Since college, she has not been unhappy with her figure or her weight.
- She is 32, unmarried, no children

Tells:

- Gives a small laugh when embarrassed, or overly nervous.

Dress:

- She usually wears a dress or skirt and blouse to work.
- Away from work, she is most often in pants and knit tops.
- She does not like high heels, wearing them only on formal occasions.
- Everything she wears must be pressed.

Family:

- both parents killed when she was 7 years old.
- Raised by her Aunt Irene and Uncle Clyde
- (Notice, I'm not going to be too picky about complete sentences, or even spelling.)

- She has one brother, 8 years older than she is. Her brother is Will Highroad, computer consultant, living in Germany.
- Aunt Irene and Uncle Clyde live in a small east Texas town, Willow Branch. Both are in their sixties, retired, travel a bit.
- Holly feels close to her aunt and uncle.
- Her brother has been gone for many years. They are good friends, but not close. He left for college when she was 10 & after college moved over seas. Visits every 2 years.

Home:

- She is buying a duplex, and she lives in one side and rents the other side to another female teacher.
- They are friendly, but each goes her own way.
- It is located in Allen, TX.

Transportation:

- She drives a four year old Ford Mustang, in excellent condition.
- Occasionally she will wash it in her driveway, but usually uses a drive-through car wash. She keeps it neat.
- Her stated policy is, if it isn't dependable, replace it.

Friends:

- Best friend is Kelly Wilson – see her minor bio.
- Has several good female friends, but they won't show up in this book – other than maybe a mention. Not in person.
- Current boyfriend is J.C. Hannery – see his bio. He would like to marry her, but she is afraid

to commit. See Psychological aspects below. They do not live together.
- Several male faculty members would like to go out with her, but for one reason or another, it doesn't happen. Perhaps J.C. puts them off when he and Holly attend some high school activity together.

Locations:

- Lived in Dallas until she was 7, then in Willow Branch (population 3,500).
- Now in Dallas suburb of Allen, Texas.

Education:

- After graduating from Willow Branch High, she attended the University of Texas in Tyler for two years, before transferring to the University of Texas in Dallas.
- Her degree was in English.
- She was a good student, graduated with honors, but doesn't recognize her intellectual ability.

Job path:

- She taught 6 years at a Dallas public high school, then moved to a private high school, St. Paul's Academy.
- Last year, she was named head of the English department at the private school.
- She is working (slowly) on a Masters of Education to further her career as a teacher.
- She declined to coach the tennis team. She told the administration she didn't have time with her advanced studies and writing, but in reality, she didn't think she could do the job well.

Summers:

- Some of the summer time is spent working on the masters degree.
- But she makes time to visit her aunt and uncle.
- She has attended several writing conferences, hoping to improve the novel she is writing and the family history she is compiling.

Likes:

- She likes country/western music, particularly Miranda Lambert.
- She likes historical romance novels, and modern romance movies. She thinks J.K. Rowling is a great writer, but she does not try to emulate her.
- Her favorite food is Italian. She continually tries to cook it with moderate success.
- Favorite dessert is gelato, followed by cannoli.

Dislikes:

- heavy metal bands
- horror movies or books
- sushi
- boxing.

Health:

- She is in excellent health.
- She plays tennis, swims, and jogs.
- She played tennis in high school. She entered a public parks tennis tournament two years ago. She lost in the first round. She decided she would stick to friendly games.

Strengths:

- She is bright
- committed to her job and her students
- loves her aunt and uncle.

Weaknesses:

- She lets people take advantage of her good heartedness.
- She is a sucker for a student with a problem. While that can be good, it also means she sometimes gets involved in problems she is ill-equipped to handle.

Goals:

- To develop some students into published writers. This is not a novel, but an article for the local newspaper, a blog post on a good website (not another kid's site), or something similar. That they can see their writing in print, that others will read it, maybe even influence some to take a stand or action. This is important to Holly. If she doesn't achieve it, she wonders about her role as a teacher.
- To publish a notable main stream novel, not to get rich, but to get a "stamp of approval".
- To have children, but only with the "right" husband/father.
- To complete a family history.

Fears:

- She fears failure, whether in her job or in her relationships.
- Part of her refusal to commit to J.C. Hannery is fear that it won't last.
- She refused to coach the tennis team for fear she would not do a good job.

Hobbies

- She likes to read
- Tennis

- writing
- She considers her work on the family history as a hobby. Her novel writing is part of her career.

How does she see herself

- She believes she is bright, but doesn't know if her personality is strong enough to influence her students to do something worthwhile.

How do others see Holly?

- Most see her as capable, bright, pleasant to be around
- But some think she is afraid to take a chance on anything, that she fears failure.
- A few are jealous that she is popular with the students.

Psychological aspects:

- Although she graduated with honors, and now heads the English department of a respected private high school, she still feels she has not proved herself.
- Publishing a successful novel is very important to her.
- Because of an unfortunate incident in college (where she was thinking marriage and he was thinking bed), she is untrusting of her feelings toward men, and cautious in her feelings towards men.

Early life episodes that influenced:

- This often includes any necessary back-story points you may need or want to include—or have for yourself for better understanding of the character.

- The death of her parents at an early age kept her childhood from being the happy, carefree time it should have been.
- The incident in college, makes her afraid to commit, afraid nothing is permanent.
- Though she lives in a Dallas suburb, she thinks of herself as a small town girl who doesn't exactly fit into the big city life.
- She gets along with friends, faculty and students, but secretly believes they view her as unsophisticated.

Significant change:

- She meets an auto mechanic, who happens to fine-tune stock cars for dirt track racing. Before the book is over, she will be racing, and winning on the dirt track. She has changed. And two of her students have published articles in the local newspaper and another has written a piece featured on the nightly local news.

That ought to wrap it up ...

Did I cover all the bases?

No. But remember, it is a dynamic work. She will change (dirt track racing?) and so will her bio.

Before we get to the minor character's bio, let me ask you a question. Do you now really know Holly?

I'm willing to say you know a lot about her. Possibly you know as much as you need to know for a book. But, could you know more? Could you know other aspects that might help if you decided to write a different novel? Or the current novel takes a turn you haven't anticipated?

Of course the answer is yes. As an example, you don't know what kind of weather she likes. Maybe she loves thunderstorms and that explains why she was out on the covered porch with a raging thunderstorm violently shaking the house and bringing down a tree that crashed on the roof of the porch and sent her to the hospital. If you want this to happen in chapter 13, then you need to let the reader know of Holly's love of thunderstorms back in chapter 4 or 5. That way, the reader is prepared. It makes sense that Holly would be out there enjoying her favorite kind of weather.

I've brought in the aspect of Holly liking or hating thunderstorms. You can think up other facets that can apply to your characters. Do not forget the opposite side of the coin: her specific, perhaps eccentric, dislikes. Remember Indiana Jones? Here is a man who braves everything, but is deathly afraid of snakes. Or the super adventurer who has claustrophobia and goes to pieces when trapped in an elevator stuck between floors.

Example: Suppose Holly is killed, apparently by a large branch falling off a tree and hitting her in the head during a thunderstorm. An unfortunate accident. But suppose you have made it clear many chapters before that Holly hates thunderstorms, is fearful of them, doesn't even stand near a window when it's lightning. The explanation that she was out in a storm will not resonate well with the police chief, or your reader, who knows Holly and her fear of storms. Sounds like a homicide to me.

Please note, you won't want to put all this information into the book. Maybe a lot of it will never appear in print. So, is it a waste to bother with it now? Not at all. It helps you understand the character better. It helps make this character a real person to you. It may provide the motivation for certain actions by the character, the person. All of this makes the work on an extensive bio well worth the time and effort. It is not time wasted. It is working to help you create a *memorable* character.

Exercise

1. Okay, don't bother to write a thousand word bio as I have above. But, sketch out a little bio for your character. If you really get into the groove, fill it out as much as you feel like.

2. How about a brief bio for the sidekick of the protagonist. You don't need as many details here. But, remember to give the sidekick something unusual. Either exaggerate some aspect of his or her character, or give this sidekick some eccentricity that will help the protagonist at some crucial point.

Chapter 9

The Black Roads

When we're traveling, I like the big, major roads. Usually on the maps, they are in red or yellow with red borders. But sometimes, to get where I want to go, I must take black roads on the map. They are the less important roads, unless they are the only ones that go where you need or want to go. And sometimes, we take the black roads because my wife wants to. She says they are more interesting than the red-bordered yellow roads, or even the red roads. Usually, she's right. So, right now, let's take the black road—not the major highway, not the protagonist or antagonist.

Here's a bio for a "middle" character in a different book I wrote. She is not the protagonist or antagonist, but is the side-kick character to the protagonist. She is quite different from the protagonist—different education, different life experiences, much different job. But through a friend of a friend, she wound up becoming a house mate for the protagonist. As the book progressed, she became an important character and her bio grew. Here is how it started out.

Example:

Bio for Brandi Brewer in *A Ton of Gold*

Roll in this book

- Brandi Brewer is the sidekick to the protagonist, Crystal Moore. She helps Crystal, and helps the author in many ways, including adding humor, bringing "street smarts" to the protagonist.

Physical

- She is 28, unmarried.
- Brandi is 5' 5" tall, 110 pounds
- Her given name was Bertha, but when she turned 21, she had it legally changed to Brandi.
- Auburn hair. Actually, it is naturally dirty blonde, but she keeps it colored at all times
- She was born with washed-out blue eyes, but wears colored contacts so that she appears to have vibrant, aqua eyes.
- She never goes out without looking her best. Careful attention to her makeup. She's pretty, but makes herself look gorgeous.

Tell, Characteristic

- She often mixes up sayings, but always has the right idea. Example: She might say, "Plagiarism is the sincerest form of flattery."

Clothes

- She has a slender and shapely build and dresses to highlight her figure.

Family

- Mother and father live in Dallas.
- No siblings. Grew up in a humble neighborhood in east Dallas.

Home

- She shares a two bedroom condo with Crystal Moore, a research computer scientist.
- The condo is in a trendy, new area of Dallas.

Friends

- She now counts Crystal as her best friend.
- She dates a detective from the Dallas Police. She claims he's the first decent man she ever dated.

Education

- Brandi finished high school as a C student.
- She doesn't consider herself smart, but she has good common sense.
- She says she has attended Street U.
- She knows how smart Crystal is, but believes herself smarter about life in the real world – on the street.

Job

- She works at an answering service
- Her hours shift from week to week.

Strength

- She has great common sense, if not book learning.
- She does not let anybody walk over her, will stand up to anybody.

Goal

- To marry and raise kids – but with the right husband. She won't settle for just anyone.

Fears

- Brandi fears little.
- But she fears going back to a life she once knew, dating scum, spending her idle time in bars.

As the novel unfolded, Brandi's bio got adjusted, expanded. For one thing, I put in the chapter in which she first appeared and where she is described.

Compare this with the bio for protagonist Holly in the previous chapter. Brandi's bio is a total of 370 words, where the bio for Holly Highroad is 1,387. Brandi plays an important role as side-kick to the protagonist in *A Ton of Gold.* The bio for a minor character that is not a side-kick might be only 100 words. The bio for the antagonist will likely fall somewhere between the lengths of the bios for the protagonist and the sidekick's—probable closer to the length of the protagonist's. In Chapter 20, we'll talk more about the very important character —the antagonist.

You will note that I have already added in several special things for Brandi. She has good common sense, she is street-wise, and she has her own version of malapropisms. These will contrast sharply with her house mate who is highly educated, is naïve in matters of the street, and would never utter a malapropism. This contrast will help define both Brandi and Crystal without my having to "tell" everything about them.

Also, you will note that she has changed herself to be the person she wants to be, rather than how she grew up. She is a person of action. She is a memorable character.

Exercise

1. If you did the exercises from the previous chapter, you have a bit of a bio for a sidekick. Having read this latest chapter, would you choose to make any changes or additions to that sidekick bio? If yes, make those changes now.

2. The antagonist is an important character (person, thing, something else). But, often an author doesn't spend that much time on a bio for the antagonist. Think of either an antagonist from your WIP or a different book and write a bio for that character. Remember, the antagonist is not 100% bad. So

include some aspect that is at least a little positive. What is the antagonist's motive? Why is he or she opposing the goal of the protagonist?

Chapter 10

Bio Templates

Because I believe in the importance and the usefulness of bios, I've included templates for a long bio and a short bio. Please feel free to copy them any way you can. Then, all you have to do is fill in the blanks, or at least many of the blanks—the more the better. Remember, it is not time wasted. It will pay off during the writing.

Here's a template for the long bio, useful for the protagonist, perhaps the antagonist, and possibly the side-kick.

Bio template for a major character

Bio for (Name) ___________
in my novel (working title)

____

Role in the book ________________
In what chapter does this character first appear? ______

In what chapter is this character described? __________
Physical Description (make this complete)

____

Characteristics, Tells, Habits, etc. (Important)

____

Clothes

____

Family

____

Health

____

Current address or living arrangement

____

Transportation ________________________________

Friends ______________________________________

Enemies ______________________________________

How does this character see herself?

____

How do others see this character?

____

Education ____________________________________

Likes ____

Dislikes ______________________________________

Strengths _____________________________________

Weaknesses ___________________________________

Goals ____

Fears ____

Hobbies ______________________________________

Psychological Aspects __________________________

Early Life Incidents ______________________________

Significant Changes ____________________________________

Other aspects that might be useful or important in the book.

____

Note that I did not specify the page number the character first appears or is described. In fact, I usually include both the chapter number and page number for my books. But, pages will be added and deleted, so that may very well change. It's also possible that chapter numbers may change, but the chapter location is more likely to remain correct. Listing where the protagonist is described physically is particularly helpful if you are writing in the first person, since the description will not likely be when the protagonist is first introduced. Be sure to note when the antagonist first shows up.

Please add in other information that might be pertinent to your character. I am not suggesting that this covers everything. It is a good start, but I encourage you to improve on it. Add in things that are unique to your characters. As I noted in chapter 8, other facets of the protagonist's personality might be worth noting. Do not be skimpy on your major characters. The more information you have in their bios, the more likely you are to make a "real" character, a more consistent character, and a memorable character.

Here is the template for a short bio. This template will not work for every one of your minor characters. Because it leaves out a lot of the items listed for the protagonist, it might leave out something important for a particular minor character. Use it only as a guideline. Adjust it as needed.

Bio template for minor character

Bio for (Name) ______________________________
in my novel (working title) ____________________
Role in the book ___________________
Chapter where this character first appear ________
Chapter where this character described ________
Physical Description ____________________________
Characteristics, Tells, Habits _______________________
Family (if important) ___________________________
Where she lives, maybe description of the place
____
Job History ____________________________________
Strengths ______________________________________
Weaknesses _____________________________________
Motives or goals (if any apparent) __________________
Connection to protagonist & antagonist (if any)
Protagonist:______________
Antagonist: ______________
Anything else that will be mentioned or play a role in the book
____

As I mentioned earlier, you can leave out any of these that do not have any effect in the book. You can and should add in any other features that impact the book. Even for minor characters, a short bio will prove helpful and will often keep you from either: spending a lot of time searching to find what you said about the person; or having some inconsistency crop up.

Bios are time well spent.

Exercise

1. Think of your WIP (Work In Progress) or your latest book. Consider what you know about your protagonist. In particular, if you have written any bio for the character, look at it. How does it compare in items of information that is in Holly's bio. Can you fill in more of the information for your protagonist that our example for Holly contains.

2. Pick out a character farther down the list. Remember the actor's adage: there are no small parts, just some with less time on stage or fewer lines. Write a small bio, less than 100 words, for such a character.

Chapter 11

You Are Pygmalion

Yes. You are.

Pygmalion is a legendary figure who carved a statue of ivory so beautiful he fell in love with it and because he loved it so much, the statue came to life.

If you love your character, the one you have carefully sculpted, the one you have created, that character *will* come alive. The character will be alive not only to you, but to your readers as well. But you must have strong feelings for the character. You must listen to the character, work to make its wishes come true. Naturally, you won't work to make the antagonist's wishes come true. But you can still have strong feelings about the antagonist.

To do this, you must know your character. And for the reader to love your character, the reader has to know your character. Keep in mind, that in the case of the antagonist, you and the reader love the way the character is crafted, how fully he is drawn, how well we know him. We can despise what he is, what he does, but appreciate how well the author (you) has allowed us to know this person.

That last sentence gives us the key. ***Person***. You, and ultimately the reader, must know this *person*. That means, the character becomes a *person*. The character is not just a description, a collection of attributes, a carefully crafted collection of words. The character comes alive, just as Pygmalion's statue came to life. The character must become a real, live *person*. You can no longer think of this as a piece of stone you have carefully carved into a statue, or a piece of canvas that you have masterfully covered with paint to become more real than the Mona Lisa. Your character is now a real person. If you can keep that frame of mind as you work with the character, the reader will come to the same position.

Not a copy ... a creation

Please note, I'm not saying model the character after a real person. I'm saying you are crafting, creating, sculpting a character so well the character *becomes* a real person.

It is because an author can deal with her characters as real people that the character can sometimes dictate where the story is going. A few years ago, Author Linda Apple wrote on Facebook that one of her characters "tapped my creative shoulder and said 'You are not finished yet. My story has to be fleshed out. You just skimmed by me and that doesn't fly with me.'" Clearly, that character was a real person to Linda, and very likely will be a real person to the reader who buys the book.

I should mention, it is *your* book. Don't let the characters take complete control of it. But be happy if the characters are talking to you, offering suggestions, having an effect on you. If that happens, you are creating characters that are "real." You are feeling it. So will the reader. But just as with kids, you are the "parent." You are in control.

Exercise

Just one exercise this chapter. But, it is important, and will take some time. Please, do not skip this one.

Spend half an hour just thinking about your character. Imagine just sitting and visiting with the character, reacting to the events of daily life (not necessarily the big "conflict" she faces), what made her laugh today, what problems (large, small, or trivial) she encountered, and what she did that she was particularly happy about.

Now, someone is saying that doesn't happen. The character only says, reacts, behaves as I, the author, tell her to. She is a puppet, only doing, thinking, saying what I tell her to. Perhaps you aren't listening to the character. The character isn't real to you. So, how can she be real to the reader? You are spending a lot of time with this character—this person. If she isn't real to you, she won't be real to the reader.

Try sitting down on the porch swing and visiting with the character. Don't dictate what she is to say. Let the character talk to you, in her words, not yours. If there are no distractions, no TV in the background, no telephone interrupting., you may be surprised at how outspoken a character can be.

Chapter 12

First Impressions

Let's believe I've convinced you that you need real people. So, how do we sculpt the character into a real person? Let's begin with something we have all heard. It refers to people, but then, our characters *are* real people. First impressions are very important. The first appearance of your character should tell us something significant about her.

Example. We might introduce a man who walks in using a cane, has a distinct limp, but his head is held high. We have subtly told the reader that this man doesn't let adversity cow him.

Example. We first meet Edward when he arrives at an estate and the butler offers to take Edward's hat and gloves. Edward ignores him completely, as if he didn't exist. This gives us a glimpse of Edward's character, and when someone later calls him Ed, and is rebuked, "My name is Edward," our opinion is reinforced.

Example. Holly first appears as she walks into a café. She speaks to the cashier and the waitress (not by name – she doesn't really know them) with a smile, arrives at the table to offer a cheery greeting not only to her friend, but also to another lady she has not met before. We could have had her arrive at the table without interaction with the cashier and waitress, speak to her friend, and wait to be introduced to the other person. But the first approach tells us a lot about Holly without our actually spelling it out for the reader. We are showing, not telling.

CLOTHES MAKE THE MAN

A person's clothes often tell us a lot about the person. She might follow the trend of the day, or she might set the trend. She might take meticulous care with her appearance, or that might be of little importance to her. You can give away a good bit about the character by telling us how she is dressed, or how she reacts to dress. Keep this in mind when writing the first appearance of the character. You can give the reader a lot of information at the onset by the way the character is dressed.

A woman dressed in chiffon and one dressed in cotton present a very different look. Does this compliment her personality? Or is this strange and perhaps uncomfortable for her?

Example: The silky material clung to every curve and garnered the attention of every male, and many of the females, in the crowded room. Jane tugged at the skirt, trying to keep it from hugging her hips. Why did she get talked into wearing this? Her blue cotton skirt and white blouse would have been more comfortable.

Does she see herself as Plain Jane?

This attention to details includes personal care, as well as clothes. Is her hair perfect in this hot, humid weather? Does she let the wind have its way with her hair? Is make-up important? Don't tell us; show us.

Example. Jennifer fished a lipstick out of her purse and with two quick motions ran a hint of pink across her lips.

Example. Ashley used a fine brush to outline her lips, opened another lipstick and brushed on a deep rose color to her lips. Finally, she applied a thin coat of gloss. She studied the effect. It's only a casual lunch. This will do.

Example. Michael checked his hair as he walked past the large mirror in the hotel lobby. Without thinking, he ran his hand over his hair, as if a strand might have the audacity to be out of place.

With a little bit of action, we have given the reader an insight into how important make-up is to Jennifer and Ashley. We don't have to tell the reader that make-up is important to Ashley and of little consequence to Jennifer.

And we've shown that Michael is very concerned with his appearance, and has been for some time. (He patted his hair without thinking.)

All of these give us a look at the person without you telling us. It's an example of the "show, don't tell" advice so often given.

Exercise

1. How will your character first appear in the book? What impression do you want to give the reader in the first sentence or two as your character arrives in the story? What information or feeling do you want to impart by the way your character is dressed? Write the first two or three sentences that introduce your character to the reader. This should be worth some of your time. Don't be satisfied with the first thing that pops into your mind.

2. Let one of your characters watch as two people enter the waiting area at the airport. Give us information on the two by the way they are dressed to show very different personalities.

3. We're still in the airport. Another person arrives. Give us a little insight on this person, not by dress, but some other aspect. If you don't know where to start, try observing the person's carry on items.

4. Write a sentence or two for the first appearance of a character that shows the reader that this character is dramatic, or shy?

Chapter 13

Motivation and Conflict

What motivates your character? This is important if we (the readers) are really going to know this person. I'm not talking about the big motivation that propels this novel along, because you will certainly make that clear. Right?

But what other motivators does this character have? What makes her get up in the morning? What makes her support some action? What compels her to take a stand on certain issues? What makes her skip dinner or lose sleep? Will all of these appear in the novel? Not necessarily. Some will show up in little scenes that add dimension to the character. But these give you, the author—Pygmalion—more insight into her character. These little bits of information will help you make the person real. And help the reader as well.

How will it help the reader? The reader is almost always able to identify with motivation. She may not know about the history surrounding the time of your novel. He may not have much feeling for the location or setting. But there is a good chance they can identify with the motivation of the character. That means they can identify with the character.

In Sol Stein's book *How to Grow a Novel,* he makes the comment that a reader can be seduced by character. But the reader will certainly need to understand and feel the motivation of the character.

Example. Charity's first pet was a dog she rescued from near death. She nursed it back to good health and she loved the dog and the dog loved her for many years. As an adult, the reader sees this kindness toward the abused, people as well as animals. You (the author) know why this is an instinct in Charity going back to her childhood. Note the choice of name here.

Example. Billie (her father wanted a boy) gets up early no matter how late she went to bed, and eats precisely at 12 noon if at all possible. Why? She was raised on a farm and no one slept past 5:30 and dinner was at 12:00, not 12:15.

Does the reader need all of this information. Maybe not. But the author does. What makes Billie tick? What makes Charity who she is?

CONFLICT

We all know that in real life conflict builds character in people. And conflict is essential to building your characters in the book. What do I mean by conflict? You already know there is some big conflict that the hero must overcome. That might be to patch up a broken family, or stop the drug lord from owning the city. It could be overcoming a life of depression. The hero will overcome this obstacle or die trying—which, by the way, is an acceptable outcome for a novel.

But what about other conflicts? There should be a plethora of them, scattered among the pages, and each tells the reader more about the character.

Example. How does Elizabeth handle the conflict with the person who pushes ahead of her in line?

Example. How does Matt handle the person who takes credit at the office for Matt's idea?

Example. How does Nicole handle a conversation when another person monopolizes it and lets no one else get a word in edgewise? Every time Nicole starts to speak, this person cuts her off with her own story. What does Nicole do, or not do.

You need to have these mini-conflicts in every chapter. Better yet, put one on every page. The conflict does not have to be big. A simple disagreement in a conversation will add a little tension to the page.

Example. "Did you hear that new song by Time Gone? Wasn't that awesome?" asked Erica.

Sophia frowned. "I heard it. Thought it was the worst song they've ever recorded."

Not a big deal. Just a little conflict. Different people have different opinions.

Wait a minute. Aren't you getting into plot here? No. The big conflict is plot. These minor conflicts flesh out your characters. And remember, plot and character are intertwined.

Exercise

1. What will motivate your character? What will be the major conflict? This is crucial to your book, so sort through a number of possibilities. Test each one. I'm not asking you to lay out the whole plot here. Just come up with a real conflict, and the motivation that drives your character. That's worth repeating. What will *drive* your character?

2. Suppose the protagonist does not want to deal with this main problem. Yes, he's the one who should solve it. Yes, he is best equipped to correct the imbalance. But, he doesn't want to be bothered. How will some characteristic (that you smoothly

slipped in much earlier) cause him to dive into finding a solution?

3. This protagonist is interested in solving the problem, whatever it may be. But he is ill-equipped to handle it. How will you, the author, slip in some quality unnoticed early in the book that will make it possible—*and believable*– for him to triumph?

4. Write just a few sentences that shows a small conflict between two characters. This is not the major conflict of the plot. Just a small conflict.

5. Write a few sentences which show why a character does some of the things she does. This can be a minor or a major character, but this is not the main motivator for solving the principal problem of the book.

Chapter 14

Do You Talk to Yourself?

Internalization is an excellent way to give the reader glimpses into what makes your character tick. Generally, a person's thoughts (private only to himself) are true indications of the makeup of the person. Private thoughts can mirror the "true" person because they *are* private. Do you have some feelings or thoughts that you do not choose to share with anyone, not your mother, not your best friend? Of course you do. It could be small, but you'd just as soon keep it to yourself. It could be as simple as thinking, *Will you shut up about your damn dog. That's all you talk about.* But you don't say it because, while you would like to hear less about the dog, this is your friend and you do not want to hurt her feelings.

In a book, you can let the reader hear those "private" revelations.

> Throughout, I will put internal thoughts in italics. That is a widely accepted method of indicating internalization.

Example. Jane stood in front of the angry man and said, "I'm sorry, but you cannot come in here." Her hands clenched into tight balls.

But do those mean she's ready to fight, or she's afraid? We're not certain. But what if she thinks, *What do I do if he pushes me aside or knocks me down and enters anyway? What can I do? There's no one to help.* Now we know; she's afraid.

Example. Mitch said, "No, no. You go ahead and take it. It's all right."

But internally he says to himself, *Go ahead, bitch. You always have to have your way.* We see, without being told, that Mitch is not as sweet and easy-going as he displays to the public.

Example. Sarah said, "Thanks, Mrs. Peters. This is really good turnip soup." She forced a smile on her face. *Just a little bit more and maybe I can leave before I throw up.*

This defines Sarah better than you telling the reader Sarah is kind to others.

Note. Internalization can *only* come from the Point Of View character. Since we are getting the story only as the POV character sees it, we certainly cannot know what is going on in someone else's mind. The POV character doesn't know what another person is thinking so cannot report on it. The POV character can imagine or guess what the other person is thinking, but she cannot know. And the reader gets the story *only* through the point of view character.

Example. Suppose Lidia is the POV character at present. Ginger is in the scene. Lidia can think, *I don't know what to say, but even as she's smiling I'm betting Ginger's mind is reading that guy the riot act.*

We know what's going on in POV Lidia's mind, but she's only guessing at what might be going on in Ginger's mind. We cannot hear Ginger's thoughts directly from Ginger.

When you change POV (say, in a new chapter) then the reader can get the thoughts (internalization) of this new POV character. Now, with this new POV character, we can no longer know the thoughts of the character who was the POV character in the last chapter, but is not the POV character now.

Bottom line: internalization can *only* come from the *current* POV character.

Internalization gives us a true picture of how the character feels about a situation or another person or an issue. Or herself. Internalization is powerful. It is a look into a person that we seldom get in real life. We don't know what the other person is thinking. But in a book, you are the creator. You can look into the mind of the character and see (actually, decide) what the person is thinking, and choose to share that with the reader. Or not.

Because internalization is so powerful, it can be overdone. You do not want the reader to be privy to every thought your character has. Pick and choose. A few well chosen bits of internalization can reveal a lot about the person. Too much and it gets tiresome.

Likewise, be careful about having access to the thoughts of too many characters. This can be confusing to the reader. Often, just the thoughts of the protagonist, and possibly the antagonist, are sufficient. As a rule (if there *were* any rules here), keep internalizations short.

Other issues (such as questions about using italics, using first person or third person, using present or past tense) when using internalization are beyond the scope of this book. Each has its advantages and disadvantages. Let's just say you should pick one method and be consistent throughout your novel. This will allow the reader to recognize internalization quickly and easily and will not be slowed down by it.

Important. You do *not* want the reader to stop and take a moment to decide what is happening right here.

So keep in mind those two caveats for internalization. It can come only from the POV character and if you use it too often, its power will be dissipated. Pick the places where it will have the most impact.

But, do use internalization. It is too powerful a writer's tool to stay in the toolbox and not be used.

I am not going to address deep POV here. The same caveats for internalization apply here. But if you have successfully employed deep POV, then no italics are needed.

Example: Wilson studied the map. I'm lost.

No need for italics or quotation marks. No need to tell the reader this is internalization —if you've clearly established this person is handled with deep POV.

Exercise

1. Think about how your *character* will use internalization. Does she encourage herself? Berate herself? Work out problems? Say to herself what she would like to say to others? Do we only see internalization when the character is under stress? Think about how you might use internalization with your character.

2. `I'm not asking you to write scenes here, and a scene is a good spot for internalization. Nonetheless, let's try a little bit. Write a very short answer the character might give to someone she meets on the street, and then a short sentence of internalization where the reader sees her contradict what she said to the person she met.

3. Let's have a character who appears to everybody to be very kind. But give us just a sentence or two of internalization that lets the reader know that in fact, he is very two-faced and might well cut you to shreds when talking with someone else.

Chapter 15

Tic, Tag, Tell

Often you will give your character some special thing that belongs to that character alone. It can be a simple mannerism, such as a slight tick in his left eye, or his perpetual half smile. **A tell** is some small thing that gives observers information about a person that the person doesn't intend to give. Captain Queeg in the *Caine Mutiny* kept two ball bearings in his pocket and as stress invaded him, he took those out and rolled them around in his hand. Author Herman Wouk doesn't have to tell us when Queeg is under stress. He just has Queeg start rolling the ball bearings in his hand and we know.

Sometimes it is a simple click of the tongue, or licking of the lips. It could be the tapping of a cane. Or the rubbing of his nose. These can be just part of the personality, or they could be (as with Queeg) an indication that something is now going on with the character.

Example: One of your characters only licks his lips when he is lying. Once this is established, you don't have to tell us he's lying. Just let that tongue come out and trace his lips. Then, we know.

Example: Wilson carries a cane with a metal tip. When he comes in, you can always hear the tap, tap, tap. Later in the story, if the reader hears the tap, tap, tap, the reader knows Wilson is coming without you having to tell the reader.

ATTITUDE

Nowadays, if you're to believe the ads, even your phone has attitude. So, what about your characters? Absolutely. For persons, this attitude is often revealed by the internalization. But since we want to limit internalization a little, what are other ways? Actual dialogue can reveal attitude. Dress or mannerisms can indicate an attitude.

Example. Give me a description of the boy with baggy pants, the crotch down to his knees, the top of his underwear showing and I know something about his attitude. I don't need internalization. If this attire is a disguise, that will need to come out. But I have the attitude he is projecting to the public.

Example. Alison walked up to Jane, who stood near the front of the long line. "Hi, Jane. I really am in a hurry. And it will only slow you down a minute if I slip in front of you. We can just visit and I'll ease in and no one will be any wiser."

Alison has an attitude. She doesn't have to take her turn in line. Her time is more important than anybody else's. And she knows Jane will not challenge her. We have learned a lot about Alison, and a little about Jane, without being told.

AN OPINION POLL

How do other characters view this person? You can reveal this in a private conversation between two other characters. It can be done during internalization, although as mentioned above, the reader has access only to the internal thoughts of the current POV character.

We all know how we see ourselves and how others see us is often quite different. That in itself is revealing. So, where appropriate, let the reader see how others view this character.

Example. "I don't know what Lauren's problem is. She is clearly the smartest one on the team, but she walks around with her head down and won't supply an opinion unless you drag it out of her."

Hopefully, the reader will see Lauren grow during the book, overcome her self-doubt induced by an oppressive father. But you didn't have to tell us she was smart; other characters did that for you.

Example. POV character is Maggie**.** Maggie smiled at John's comment about Lauren. *Lauren is so much smarter than John it isn't even funny*.

Since Maggie is the POV character, we know the internalization comes from her, and now we know how she feels about John.

Exercise

1 – 3. This is a three part exercise. Put down one "tell" for your character. Describe in one sentence her attitude. Again in one sentence, how do others view her?

For the last two, I've said use one sentence. When you are ready to use this character in a book, you may want to have several sentences for each of these. Probably you still want only one "tell."

4. Pick a different character in your WIP. Then give this person a tell that you can use throughout the book.

5. Show us something about a high school student's attitude by having him interact with another high school student who is stocking shelves in the local food store. Don't let the first student be even slightly rude. But let his attitude be clear.

Chapter 16

The Fourth Dimension

Everybody talks about developing a three dimensional character. What are those three dimensions? Writers can give you a variety of descriptions for these. They might be: physical, mental, emotional. Or Maryann Dioro calls them: surface, soul, and spirit. However you want to describe it, the end result is a well-rounded character, where the reader can know what the character looks like, how the character acts, where the character came from, what the character really thinks, and what the character really feels.

There's a lot to be said for that. But, I'm going to ask you to develop *four*-dimensional characters. Take all that is said about three dimensional characters and then add in a fourth dimension: the time factor. Your character needs to change over time. Many writers and books refer to this as the character arc. I call it the fourth dimension.

How do you accomplish this? You develop your three dimensional character, much as I've discussed already. Then you add on top of that - change. This can be gradual across the entire book. This is perhaps the more usual approach. The character slowly moves from point A (some belief or behavior) to point B. This may, in fact, be the major conflict I talked about. Change is often difficult. The character resists this change. But slowly, the change occurs. This provides a classic character arc, or fourth dimension. The final scene will often consist of the character thinking about how he or his life has changed. And he can be happy about it, or disappointed, or simply accepting.

Example: Scarlett O'Hara, in *Gone With the Wind,* desperately wants Ashley. It is only at the end of the book that she realizes Ashley is not what she wanted at all.

Example: What about the change in Ebenezer Scrooge in Charles Dickens's *A Christmas Carol*? He definitely changes with time.

The change can be a bit more compressed, perhaps even sudden. An event or situation is sufficiently traumatizing that a significant change in the character occurs. This can affect the character, someone the character feels strongly about (loves or hates), or some cause or thing the character cares about.

Example. A person is killed as a direct or indirect result of the position your character holds onto stubbornly. Your character sees that his previous stance was not worth the cost. Never again will he let such a belief become a serious problem for others.

Regardless of the approach you take, some of your characters need to change during the course of the book. Major changes, minor changes, slowly, suddenly, you have choices. But change must occur.

Example. In my book ***A Ton of Gold*** the protagonist is a very bright young woman who has been psychologically brutalized by a university professor. Now, the mere mention of his name causes her immediately to lose all self-confidence. But other things happen to her and by the end of the book, she is able to see him for what he is, and has gained the strength to stand up to him even as he tries to emotionally abuse her again. She has changed over time. She can now fight back. She is a four dimensional character.

Example. In the children's book *Sarah, Plain and Tall,* author Patricia MacLachlan develops a great character in Sarah who comes to the Midwest as a mail-order bride to help raise two motherless children. She grows homesick for the Maine sea shore and finds the dust storms intolerable. But over time, Sarah comes to love the children, and the father, and in the end even the Midwest farm life. She changes slowly over time. She is a four-dimensional character.

Exercise

1. How will *your* character change over some time period? This time period might be years, weeks, days or the course of the book. Tell us what changes in the character, and over what time period.

2. Tell us about how a character might change in a matter of minutes, or even seconds. What could bring about such a sudden change.

Chapter 17

Two Caveats

Tighten the Purse Strings.

Not all the things we have talked about should be applied to all characters. Everything that goes into the character bio does not need to go into the book. In fact, your bio should contain some information for you alone. While it will not go into the novel, it will help color the character.

Naturally, this applies differently to different characters. Some have small bios and most of that will be used in the book. Your protagonist and antagonist, even the sidekick, will have significant bios and it is possible that a good bit will not be spelled out in the book.

Don't tell everything you know.

All of it may influence how you treat the character. It may have a bearing on how the character is presented to the reader. But it does not all have to be spelled out to the reader. Perhaps the astute reader will infer some of the information you have withheld. That's fine. Actually, that's better than fine. It means you have done a good job of making your character a real person. Congratulations.

Forget Everything I've Said?

There are times and characters where you do not want to spell out who they are, where they came from, what they think, or where they're going. This is an unusual approach and you need to think it through very carefully before using this approach. But there are some stories where this is appropriate. The event of the story is so dominant that you, the author, do not want the character intruding. You have decided that any additional information on the character is not necessary to your story. More than just not necessary, you have decided it will interfere with the story.

This is not a usual or easy approach. I would caution the writer to use this only after careful consideration. You are giving up much. The reader has little chance to identify with or become connected with your character. The goal of this book is to help you create *memorable* characters. It will prove difficult to make such a character by withholding all information on the character.

However, there are stories (perhaps not books) that can benefit from this approach.

Exercise:

It's a holiday. No exercise for this chapter.

Chapter 18

Talk, Talk, Talk

Dialogue? Or Dialog? Whichever, what is it doing in here?

We all know that dialogue is a very important part of a novel. In fact, poor dialogue can ruin an otherwise good book. Some authors handle it very well, and even some published authors do not. Many a manuscript has been turned down strictly on the basis of poor dialogue. James Lee Burke is considered a master of dialogue. I like Dick Francis for dialogue that reads very smoothly. And the late Elmore Leonard was widely recognized for having a great talent for dialog.

Good dialogue is not all that easy. Teaching it, or guiding one through it, is worth its own book. In fact, (a very brief commercial) I have a book devoted to dialog, titled ***How to Write Great Dialog***. The third edition was released in September, 2021.

Still, I haven't explained why this alien is lurking in a Character Development book. Dialogue can tell us a great deal about a character. It can give us clues to where this character grew up. Someone raised in Boston will speak rather differently than one raised in Atlanta. Professor of Phonics Henry Higgins (in *Pygmalion* or *My Fair Lady*) claimed to be able to tell where a person came from, within a few miles, just by listening to that person's speech. I have my doubts about that, but it made a good story. (Remember, we exaggerate the character.) However, between Texas and Minnesota? No doubt.

Dialogue can tell us about the educational level of the character. A college professor and a grade school dropout may have been raised and lived their entire lives in the same town, but their speech will be different. On the other hand, a person *can* chose to change that early indoctrination. With study and practice, speech patterns can be completely changed. It is not easy, and in periods of stress, often the old speech pops out. That in itself might be an interesting point in a book. A spy is uncovered, or a woman who is trying to hide her past has it revealed, when in a stressful situation those early life speech patterns pop out.

Dialogue can tell us about the attitude of a person. We've all heard a person speak and immediately thought, there's a valley girl, or he's a gang member, or he's trying to move in circles he is not accustomed to, or he would like to sound tougher than he is. No description was necessary, just a bit of dialogue.

A person can have different modes of speech. The teenager might have different speech patterns and vocabularies for class, for home and for friends. A man may have a different way of talking at the office, at the gym, and at home. Imagine a high powered executive addressing the board of directors, then going home and playing with his young children. It would be strange and unnerving if the man spoke to his young children in the same manner that he spoke to the board of directors. And he wouldn't last long as CEO if he addressed the board in the same fashion as he did his five year old twins. This would be part of the four dimensional character – different dialogue patterns for different times.

Accomplishing this in a smooth manner is not easy to do. Most of the time it is not needed. But if it is needed, it will give the reader some real insight into the character and will be worth the effort. Let's revisit the high powered executive. What would it tell you about him if he addresses his young children in the same tone and manner he addresses the board of directors? If he does, that could be an important point in the story, possibly the most important point. And maybe we will see him change during the book and find a way to communicate and bond with his children, as well as with the board of directors.

A word of caution. Too much dialect or odd speech patterns can be damaging. It quickly gets tiresome for the reader to plow through our attempt at phonetically trying to capture a dialect. So, what do you do? You give us just a taste at the beginning. Then, you throw in subtle reminders from time to time.

Example. "Jeremy, where on earth did you learn to talk that way?" "Was raised in the Blue Mountains. Didn't go to school 'til I was near twelve."

Example. After Derrick left the room, Kyle said, "Do you have as much trouble understanding him as I do? It's not just the choice of words. Half the time it's the way he mangles them."

Like cayenne pepper, use dialect cautiously.

So, what's the bottom line? Consider that dialogue has two jobs. The first is, of course, to convey some information. The second is to *show* us something about a character, without *telling*.

BODY LANGUAGE

"Good grief, I'm still struggling with dialogue and now you want to talk about body language."

Remember that words are only a small part of the way we communicate with one another.

Body language can tell us a lot about a character and a character's state of mind at the moment. Often the person doesn't intend to provide this information. She may even specifically think that she will not reveal this feeling. But her body conveys the information just as clearly as if she spoke it.

Example: A man is chatting up a woman at a party. She crosses her arms across her chest. He might as well move on. Her body language says she is shutting him out.

Example. Many psychologists will interpret a woman running her fingers around the edge of her cocktail glass as a sexual sign.

Example. A man who walks into a room with his head held high and his shoulders back shows people he is confident – without ever saying a word.

Example. When he's talking with a woman, Mark might lean ever so slightly toward her. This shows that he has no other concern than her.

The use of body language is an excellent way of showing not telling.

Like spoken dialogue, the study of body language requires a book (or two or three) to be adequately covered. I won't try to do that here. But keep body language in mind. Sprinkle just a little here and there to help make your character a real person, maybe one with fidgeting hands that show his nervousness.

Exercise

1. This doesn't have to be about your chosen character, but give an example (that you *might* use for some character) of a speech pattern that will tell us a lot about the character's

educational background without you having to spell it out for us. This could be the extent of her education or the character's participation in the process.

2. Come up with one piece of body language that will tell the reader something about your character.

3. Pick a character from something you have written and let his language show the reader where he was raised. This could be the part of the country, or the type of neighborhood in which he was raised.

Chapter 19

The Same – Not

Without meaning to, both you and I have probably thought of most of this discourse thus far as pertaining to the protagonist. Maybe even his sidekick. But what about the antagonist?

For some reason, it seems all too easy to build a nice three dimensional (and now, we'll build a four dimensional) character for the protagonist. And in the same book, we cut out a pasteboard antagonist. Just give the reader a Flatland character who is evil and – well really, what else do you need to know about him. He's bad.

Wrong.

If you don't have a strong, well defined antagonist, then your protagonist has nothing to work against. In a blog, I once gave this analogy. The University of Texas traditionally has a powerful football team. But generally they open their season against a small, weaker opponent. That gives the coaches a chance to see what they've got, to iron out any wrinkles, to get their players in a groove against an easy team. But, there is no excitement to that game. There is no doubt what the outcome will be. There is no suspense, no tension. It is, generally, boring, unless you're a die-hard Longhorn fan who doesn't care about the score as long as the men in burnt-orange win.

The legendary Indian warrior Crazy Horse said, **"You are only as strong as your enemy."**

Let's hear it for the bad guy …

You don't want your readers to feel the protagonist has no opposition. The reader probably believes, even with a tough antagonist, that the protagonist will come out on top in the end. That does not have to be the case. But even if the reader is right and the protagonist is going to come out on top, the reader does not know what it will cost the protagonist. The reader doesn't know how the protagonist will be changed, perhaps for life, or what collateral damage there might be. Nor does the reader know how or when.

All of these things create suspense. Give the protagonist an antagonist that is much weaker, much dumber, much less driven and the suspense disappears. You must make the reader think that this time, the protagonist is going to lose. It does happen. And this might be the time. Or the protagonist will survive, but she will lose something or someone very important to her.

What this means is that you need to pay as much attention to your antagonist as you do to your protagonist. Okay, maybe not exactly the same amount, but close.

One way to do this is to imagine that you are a really bad guy and you are going to make the antagonist the hero. The antagonist is going to win. Oh, he is still a bad guy, but you like bad guys – are one yourself.

Show us the world through the antagonist's eyes, see his motivation, his emotions, and you will make him more realistic and that will make him more formidable and scarier.

If you crafted this story from the other side of the fence, how would you build your antagonist? You would make him (or her) a four dimensional character, using all the things I've mentioned in the previous chapters. Yes, four dimensional. The bad guy can change, have a character arc. Often in books that is not the case. But why not? In fact, the bad guy could start out on the other side, and something happens to suck him into the dark side.

Example: The antagonist, Mr. Bender, starts out an okay guy. But he makes a mistake. Not a road-to-hell mistake. Still, because of his family he decides he must break into a store and destroy the evidence. It's not a big deal. It was a small mistake. But while he is in there, a guard comes in and finds him. Still not willing to accept his mistakes, Bender grabs something off the desk to knock the guard out so he can escape. Unfortunately, the paperweight is very solid and heavy, and the guard is killed. Now, with a murder rap hanging over Bender, he will do anything to anybody to avoid getting caught. Bender has become a genuine bad guy and the guard will not be the last person he will kill. Bender has changed over time. Bender has a distinct character arc. Bender can be a four dimensional character.

My character is tougher than your character ...

Often, you will want the antagonist to be stronger and smarter than the protagonist. In fact, it looks like there is no way the protagonist can win. The reader says, "Well, this is one of those novels where the protagonist dies trying. The protagonist is putting up a good fight, but she is outgunned. She will lose. I hate that. I really liked her. Put up a memorial to her." But lo and behold, the protagonist wins. How is this possible? Perhaps the protagonist is more driven, more passionate. Or she could be more inventive.

I try to avoid having her just be lucky. The reader can feel cheated if it is just luck that saves the heroine. To avoid this, set in place *early in the book* the facts that will lead to the defeat of the antagonist at the end. Give the protagonist the tools that will be needed, and give the antagonist the flaw that will lead to his defeat.

Example: We learn early in the book, when it raises no flags, that the antagonist is very smart, very strong, and very confident. In fact, over-confident. At the crucial point, the protagonist is able to use this over-confidence against the antagonist and defeat him.

Being able to use the antagonist's strength to cause his downfall is an excellent gambit. It is one that can be used more often than you might think. Each strength can also be an Achilles heel that the protagonist can attack.

Hired Gun ...

Your antagonist may be a killer for hire. You might think that there is little you can do to flesh out this character. Not so. You begin with his bio. How did he get into this trade? Could be an interesting story right there. Did he seek it, or did the jobs find him? What does he do when he is not out killing someone? What is his attitude toward his victims? Does he ever feel remorse? Are there some jobs he will not take? How long ago and how many times has he said, "This is my last job." Does he have a family? Everybody has *some* family. What is his? Do they know what he does? If they are aware of his work, do they care?

Do you see where I'm going? You can make as extensive a bio for the antagonist as for the protagonist. In striving for the four dimensional character, the antagonist must have some redeeming quality. Rarely do we have a person who is one hundred percent evil. At the very least, he wasn't always that way. Now, we have that fourth dimension. He has changed from law abiding to criminal, from bad to evil. This change can make for an interesting plot point. Why or how did he move to the dark side?

As I said above, you can, and must, make the antagonist a worthy opponent for the protagonist. Otherwise, your protagonist is going to be uninteresting. Why bother rooting for her? She has no real challenge. It would be like the protagonist winning a race when she was the only contestant. Why bother to have the race? She's gotten a free ride. And your reader will be bored.

Exercise

1. Think of some way that the antagonist is better, smarter, stronger than the protagonist. Then imagine how that very strength of the antagonist will provide the way the protagonist achieves her goal.

2. Take a protagonist, one who doesn't seem cut out to be a hero, to defeat a very capable antagonist. But, early in the book, give this character some little talent, perhaps an unusual talent. But in the end, that talent is just what is needed to defeat the antagonist. What? No, I didn't say it was an easy assignment. But, properly done, it can turn a so-so story into one people talk about—a story that is the talk of the town, and happens to sell thousands of copies. Maybe it's worth a little time.

3. Let's say the antagonist is color blind. We know that, incidentally (no big deal) from the beginning. Now, when the big climax arrives in your book, it turns out that being able to recognize various colors is necessary. Our otherwise impenetrable antagonist is now in trouble, and the protagonist takes advantage of it to defeat the bad guy. Decide how that small problem for the antagonist leads to his defeat.

Chapter 20

The Antagonist is Missing!

I can't find the antagonist, oh my.

Can you have a protagonist without an antagonist? Yes and no. (That ought to cover it.)

The "no" part says you must have an opposing force of some sort, which we normally call the antagonist. The protagonist has a goal and someone or something is trying to prevent the protagonist from achieving that goal.

The "yes" part says, it does not have to be a human. An alien? A robot? An energy field? No. All of those can be thought of in the same light as the human antagonist. This is clearly the case with the alien. It (or should that be "he" or "she") is a life force that maybe we're not familiar with, but a life force nonetheless. The robot? Typically in this situation, the robot is made or programmed to act at least somewhat like a human. Think of HAL 9000 in the movie "2001: A Space Odyssey." Okay, HAL was a computer, but that's close enough. A robot is, after all, mainly a computer. HAL just couldn't move.

> Here is an aside. Many people thought the name HAL was derived from taking IBM and backing up one spot for each letter. The I moved back to H; B moved back to A; and M moved back to L. The official word was that HAL came from **H**euristic **AL**gorithm. A . Heuristic algorithm would be the way the

computer (HAL) was programmed, or instructed to function.

HAL becomes a formidable antagonist and kills most of the crew. Only Frank Bowman manages to escape and disable HAL. The American Film Institute listed HAL as the thirteenth greatest film villain. Clearly we can have robots or machines as antagonists.

How about the energy field? Even the energy field is given human qualities.

All of those instances mean we have an antagonist to oppose the protagonist. Then, what does the "yes" part really mean.

I'm my own worst enemy ...

The problem that the protagonist has to overcome may be herself. The protagonist and the antagonist are two sides of the same person. If this were a case of multiple personalities, then we might put this up with the other villains. The protagonist is personality A and the antagonist is personality B. But let's say it is not a case of multiple personalities, but a weakness in the protagonist. For instance, the struggle is to overcome extremely low self esteem.

Well, that ought to be easy.

Not necessarily.

If this low esteem has been hanging around for ten years, it could be a very difficult, perhaps impossible, task to overcome. Could this be sufficient for a book? Yes it can, and it has been done many times.

It's true that often this low self esteem was induced by another person, perhaps a parent. That could be part of the back story that is never addressed in the book. The author may concentrate her efforts on the protagonist's struggle to overcome this problem, and not spend any time on where it originated.

How does this bare on the subject of this book?

It means that the author must make the character of the protagonist even better. There is no antagonist to play against, thus the protagonist must carry the entire load. The reader must feel the pain of the protagonist, identify with it, strain to help the protagonist overcome it. Instead of thinking this is easier since the author doesn't have to create a substantial character to oppose the heroine or hero, the author must redouble her efforts to make the reader engage with the protagonist. This is not always easy. Depending on the situation, it is possible that the reader will simply say to the protagonist, "Get over it; quit whining; get a life." You, the author, must draw the reader in to sympathize with the protagonist, and truly pull for the protagonist to succeed.

The protagonist might be trying to deal with an addiction to gambling, drink, drugs, etc. Now, you might think that the alcohol is the antagonist. But in reality, it isn't the bourbon or the scotch. It is the sickness of the protagonist that has to be overcome. It isn't the roulette wheel or the card table that must be overcome; it is the character's weakness.

Your job may be easier with a clear cut antagonist. But it can be rewarding to make the story work without one.

Exercise

1. Imagine a non-human antagonist. It could be a virus, an alien, a personality flaw in the protagonist. Then, briefly, set up the confrontation between your character you've been working on and this new antagonist. What special features does this antagonist need to appear real to the reader?

2. Having selected a non-human antagonist, how will your character deal with the threat? When does the protagonist recognize the true nature of this “antagonist”? Is that the same time the protagonist makes the decision to confront this problem? Or does it take some time after recognizing the problem for the protagonist to understand that he or she must deal with it?

Chapter 21

Unsung Heroes

Secondary characters, sidekicks and minor parts...

I've talked about the protagonist and antagonist. Yes, it's true, you could have a book with only two characters. *The Road,* by Cormac McCarthy, has only two characters (and neither is given a name). But that's unusual. I wouldn't recommend trying that until you have a very large and loyal fan base.

It works well for the protagonist to have *somebody.* This is usually a friend, although it could be a stranger whom the protagonist happens to meet and who impacts the protagonist in some way. It could be a minor adversary who prepares, or influences the protagonist in her battle with the antagonist. It could even be imaginary, as is the case in *Harvey.* Elwood P. Dowd has an imaginary friend Harvey, who happens to be a six foot tall rabbit that only Elwood can see or hear. Author Mary Chase brings this off very well and by the end of the play, you can believe in Harvey, even if you can't see him. (It became a very popular movie with Jimmy Stewart playing Elwood P. Dowd.)

The work you put into this sidekick character, depends on how extensively you use him or her (or it). Keep in mind that, as with music or painting or any art form, it is often the nuances that set it apart. (Do not forget that writing is as much an art form as any of the others. Never let the literary arts be treated as the step-child of the arts.) Give the sidekick ample attention. Make up the bio. Let the character percolate in your brain, not as long as the time given to the protagonist and the antagonist, but ample time.

The sidekick can sometimes receive as much attention from the reader as the protagonist. You'd like to avoid that. The sidekick is, after all, the sidekick, not the main character. Make sure that the protagonist is clearly the center of attention.

The Lone Ranger wasn't alone ...

If you're not convinced about the importance of the sidekick, try to imagine Batman without Robin. Or Superman without Lois Lane. The green Hornet without Kato. One of my favorites was The Lone Ranger with his sidekick Tonto. And who could forget Margo Lane, the "constant companion" of Lamont Cranston, The Shadow - *who knows what evil lurks in the hearts of man*. Was much thought put into developing the character of Margo Lane? You bet. She appeared in more than fifty Shadow novels, and in the 1994 film with Alex Baldwin. Margo (played by Penelope Ann Miller) is a principal character in the film.

Many of the same items you determined for the protagonist and the antagonist should be written down for the sidekick. What is the sidekick's motivation? It might be simply to help the protagonist. But a separate goal that ties in neatly with the plot will certainly make for a more interesting character and thus improve the book. This can be a bit tricky as you do not want to have this goal overshadow or impact the goal of the protagonist.

Easier is to have the sidekick have a separate *motive*. This may be known only to the sidekick and the reader. It spurs the sidekick to help the protagonist even more, because when the protagonist succeeds, the sidekick will fulfill his motive also. Or the sidekick's motive might be revealed to the protagonist near the end of the book. The secret motive for the sidekick can add another level of interest to the book.

Example: The protagonist's *goal* is to discredit Mr. Badner who is running for governor. The protagonist's *motive* is that Badner was the direct cause of the protagonist losing his business and reputation as a young man. The sidekick joins in to help discredit Badner. So, he has the same goal. But the sidekick's motive is very different. He wants to avenge the rape of his sister by Badner. The sidekick may never tell the protagonist. Or he might. The author decides.

Let the sidekick have his or her own tell. Let the sidekick have his own personality. Let the sidekick be identified on her own, not simply as "friend of the protagonist."

Generally, you don't want the sidekick to be a mirror image of the protagonist. You'd like not to have the sidekick be a "yes man." Don't have the sidekick follow every step the protagonist takes, agree with every action the protagonist makes. On the contrary, the sidekick should be in disagreement with the protagonist often. They might argue. They might part company and for a short while, go their separate ways. Remember, we want to add little conflicts as often as possible. In the end, the sidekick is there to help the protagonist or at the very least, share in the joy that the antagonist has been defeated.

It is okay for the protagonist to take advice from the sidekick. Make the sidekick an independent, interesting person. Often, the sidekick character doesn't have the qualities to ever be the protagonist. The sidekick could not carry the fight to the antagonist. But the sidekick can be an important help to the protagonist one way or another.

Just how strong are you? ...

On the other hand, it is also possible that were the protagonist not around, the sidekick could take over that job.

That is, you've made the sidekick a stronger person. But, this is a struggle between the protagonist and the antagonist. As the protagonist will probably say, "This is my fight. I have to deal with it." The sidekick can be a strong character and could be a protagonist, just not in this book. The protagonist is here and takes center stage. The sidekick helps focus the spotlight on the protagonist.

In my book *A Ton of Gold,* I pair a street-wise high school graduate with a near-Ph.D. research computer scientist. I highlight the differences throughout the book. This contrast helps emphasize features of the protagonist that I want to underscore without my beating the reader over the head. By juxtaposing the two, I can *show* features without having to *tell* the reader. And it is this "opposite type" character who allows the protagonist to find her way to the solution – well, at least for the subplot.

It is possible that the problem with the antagonist actually comes through the sidekick. The protagonist feels she must step in to help her out-gunned friend. Usually, this is not at the request of the sidekick. In fact, the sidekick may tell the protagonist to stay out of it. The protagonist, seeing that the sidekick cannot win, steps in to carry the fight to the antagonist.

Can you have more than one sidekick? Certainly. But be careful in this area. Too many can distract from the protagonist. And I believe there is a tendency with multiple sidekicks not to develop any of them fully. Make as many sidekicks as you *need*; no more.

Too many crooks can spoil the book ...

Can the antagonist have a side-kick? Certainly. This is not done as often. Clearly, if the identity of the antagonist is not revealed until late in the book, having a sidekick for the antagonist could be tricky. You might give away the identity of the antagonist. But, with care, you can do it. If the antagonist is known early on, giving that character a sidekick should be no problem. This is not the usual approach as it shines more light on the antagonist, possibly taking away from the protagonist. However, in some books, the antagonist is an equal player with the protagonist, gets as much ink, and can have his own sidekick.

In an early manuscript of mine, part way through I discovered that the sidekick was taking over the show. This is not as unusual as it might seem. In fact, it's easy. You find you can make the sidekick a quirky person, with loads of personality, and the sidekick is not hampered by having to move the plot along as stringently as the protagonist must.

At that point, what were my choices? One, tone down the sidekick. Relegate him or her back to the role of sidekick, not the main attraction. Two, rewrite the book and turn the sidekick character into the protagonist. Remember, you want the reader to identify with, sympathize with, root for, and be very involved with ... the protagonist. The sidekick is to help this happen, not take the gold medal.

The main point here is this. *The sidekick character is not an afterthought.* The sidekick is not something thrown in to add words or simply to describe your main character. This character should not be considered a second class citizen. The sidekick should add a nuance to your book, lifting it up to another level. That means, you give the sidekick the care and attention necessary to produce a *memorable* character.

A Helping Hand

The sidekick has another characteristic, one that is important to the writer. The sidekick can be as much help, perhaps even more help, to *you*, the author. Why is that? The sidekick allows easy access to bring into the book things the author wants that may not come easily from the protagonist.

Example: Humor. The protagonist may be very serious, straight-laced, maybe not much "fun." He or she has a lot on her mind. Perhaps her goal weighs heavily on her. You the author needs some levity; the reader needs a break.

Enter the sidekick. The sidekick doesn't have this pressure or this obsession about the "goal." So the sidekick is happy to be crazy, funny, a prankster, whatever the author wants or needs. The sidekick can drag the protagonist into a funny scene, one the protagonist would never investigate on her own.

Because the sidekick doesn't have the same drive to "right this wrong," the sidekick has the time, and inclination, to pursue other interests. This allows the author to introduce additional topics, scenes, ideas without diluting the protagonist's character.

In short, the sidekick is a great help to the writer. There is no doubt in my mind that a sidekick makes the life of the author easier. Need to save the protagonist when things aren't going well? Bring in the sidekick who can either help the protagonist get out of a tight situation (either adding muscle, wit, or ideas), or defuse the atmosphere allowing for an easy exit.

It's almost like the magician pulling a rabbit out of the hat. The author is in a tough bind. How to get out of this spot? Aha! In walks the sidekick and the situation is saved.

The sidekick is more of a friend to the author than he is to the protagonist. The sidekick may help the protagonist solve the problem or achieve the goal. But the sidekick will be a savior over and over for the writer.

Exercise

1. A few exercises back, I asked you to conjure up a sidekick for your protagonist. Think of a motive, different from the motive of the protagonist, that the sidekick might have to help the protagonist achieve her goal.

2. What about a different goal for the sidekick, but one that would mesh with that of the protagonist? This is a little trickier, but satisfying.

3. Give an example where the sidekick can enter a scene just in time to prevent the protagonist from being overwhelmed by the antagonist. This does not have to be a physical situation, although it could be. But maybe the timing is not right to try to achieve the book's "goal," just yet.

4. Construct a scene where things are getting too serious and leading to a confrontation (for which you, the author, are not ready for yet). Let the sidekick introduce humor into the scene and defuse the problem.

5. Set up a scenario where the sidekick character is unknown to the protagonist prior to a situation in which a stranger (to become the sidekick) helps the protagonist. It could be that things are getting too tense between the protagonist and the antagonist and this stranger steps in with a joke to avert a confrontation. And after that, this new person becomes a valuable sidekick to the protagonist.

Chapter 22

But the Plot?

So, we're just forgetting about plot?

No, not at all. But, plot isn't the subject of this book.

However, since you brought it up, character can *be* the plot.

Say what?

It is possible to make the character sufficiently convoluted that the plot of the book is unraveling the character. There might be a little window-dressing, but the engine of the book (the plot) is understanding this character. So all of the ingredients you have woven into the character actually make up the plot.

This is not easy to sustain throughout a book. It is more likely to happen in a short story. But a skillful writer can reveal the character in stages and work toward an understanding of the character in a way that draws the reader in, involves the reader, and maintains the reader's interest for eighty thousand words. Some biographies take this form. It is the character, not the action, which forms the "plot."

Examples: Here are some examples in famous works of fiction that do this:

John Steinbeck's *Of Mice and Men*
Toni Morrison's *The Bluest Eye*;
Ray Bradbury's *Fahrenheit 451.*

In Bradbury's book, Guy Montag is the central character and it is his slow change that is important. Yes, there are the book burnings. But the book is about Montag and his change, aided by a young girl who tells him about the past, and a professor who tells him about the future. Montag *is* the plot, not the fires.

I've mentioned earlier that the protagonist can be his own worst enemy. The antagonist can be some facet of the protagonist. The obstacle the protagonist must overcome is himself, or some characteristic of himself. We've seen the movies where there is a powerful evil force threatening the protagonist. In the end, it turns out that the evil force is within the protagonist, some aspect of the protagonist's personality or being.

This type book requires a very deep and careful analysis of the main character. The author must know, or come to know, every small detail of the character's makeup. In these books, character is king. And character is the plot.

Exercise

1. Imagine a protagonist who has a personality quirk that would require a book to straighten out. Could this hold the interest of the reader for 80,000 words? Okay, 65,000 words? Can you name a book that succeeded in maintaining your interest where the antagonist was simply a part of the protagonist's makeup?

Chapter 23

The Final Word

I've concentrated on character in this book. I've recommended ways to set up your characters, how to give them a back story, a history. I' made suggestions on how to flesh out the characters, to make them real, three dimensional. I've even recommended that you strive for *four* dimensional characters, showing how they evolve over time. This is what books mean when they talk about the character arc. At least some of your characters must change from the beginning of the book to the end. In some instances, all the characters are changed, some less than others, but changed nonetheless.

Your job is to make certain that the reader experiences that change. You do not want to have your readers sitting on the sideline and watching pictures go by, even if they admire them. You must get the readers inside the story. You must strive to make the readers identify with the protagonist. If the protagonist is hurt, your readers must feel that. When the protagonist is overcome by happiness, your readers must be smiling. If the protagonist is worried or fearful, you'd like for the readers to be nervous. The protagonist is laughing? The readers should be laughing. And when the protagonist achieves her goal, the readers should feel a sense of accomplishment, feel relaxed and content that the obstacles have been overcome.

To do this you need a character so real that the reader thinks of her as a friend, a close friend, one whose hopes and dreams become the reader's.

If the protagonist is in trouble, the reader should not be able to put the book down until the reader has helped the protagonist get out of the bad situation.

Am I asking too much? I think not. Consider some book you really enjoyed. Remember the protagonist in that book. Did you feel for him? Did you pull for him to win? Did you try to tell him when he was about to get into trouble, warn him when the antagonist was about to attack? Probably you did. That's the kind of involvement you'd like to create with your characters – to make the reader care. To make the characters memorable.

For the reader, it's simple.

No tears? No laughter? No good.

Give your readers *memorable* characters that they care about.

Exercise

Write a book with truly memorable characters. Start now. Send me a copy when you finish. I'll write a review for it.

James R. Callan

How to

Write

GREAT

Dialog

Pennant Publishing

Shows how to:

- ✓ Develop Characters through Dialog
- ✓ Further the Plot with Dialog
- ✓ Establish Relationships between Characters
- ✓ Create Tension and Conflict using Dialog
- ✓ Build a Dialog Signature for Major Characters
- ✓ Handle Attributions to Improve Dialog
- ✓ Learn the Power of Internal Dialog and the Restrictions
    - PLUS More!

"As an editor, I wish all my clients would read and apply the advice in this book. James Callan describes the writing of dialog in simple terms, easy to grasp and apply. Highly recommended."
Lorna Collins, content editor

"Callan's easy to understand explanations and variety of exercises make this how-to perfect for the novice, as well as the seasoned writer."
Michelle J.G. Perin, PSWA Writing Competition Chair

"A REALLY HELPFUL book ...will teach you 'everything you need to know about writing dialog'... along with very practical advice..."

Arlene Uslander, professional editor

"This book should be in every aspiring writer's library. Writing believable dialog that adds to the storytelling and lets the reader know something about the character is what makes or breaks a novel. Excellent advice."

F. M. Meredith, author of *Murder in the Worst Degree*

About the Author

James R. Callan took a degree in English, intent on writing. But when that did not support a family, he returned to graduate school in the field of mathematics. Upon graduation, he worked as a research mathematician, segueing into computer science, and a thirty year detour from writing.

Along the way, he received grants from the National Science Foundation, NASA, and the Data Processing Management Association. He has been listed in *Who's Who in America, Who's Who in Computer Science*, and *Two Thousand Notable Americans.*

Then one day, he realized his children were grown, out of college and self-supporting. He could return to his original love—writing. For two years, Callan wrote a monthly column for a national magazine. For six months, he wrote a weekly column that appeared in newspapers in four states. Callan has had fourteen books published: five non-fiction books, plus nine mystery/suspense novels. All of the novels appear in print, audio, and e-book formats. The audio version of one of his books rose as high as number seven on the publisher's list. He has had shorter works published in five anthologies, and was the editor for another anthology. He also gives workshops on various aspects of writing in the U.S., Mexico and on the Internet. He can be contacted through his website: www.Jamesrcallan.com .

He and his wife split their time between homes in east Texas and Puerto Vallarta, Mexico. They have four children and seven grandchildren.

www.ingramcontent.com/pod-product-compliance
Ingram Content Group UK Ltd.
Pitfield, Milton Keynes, MK11 3LW, UK
UKHW041852190726
13854UKWH00002B/846

9 798201 293376